Space Chase

Book 4:

THE MECHANIZER

By Dr Joe

Cover art by Dr Joe

National Library of Australia Cataloguing-in-Publication entry

Author:	Ireland, Joe, author.	
Title:	Space Chase 4: The Mechanizer	
Series:	Space Chase	
Imprint:	Dr Joe.	
ISBN:	9780648494164	
Date:	15 December 2019	
Pages:	168	
Target Audience:	Young adult / Primary school.	
BISAC:	EDU029030	Education, teaching materials
Dewey Number:	813	F IRE
Lexile Number:	750	

All characters appearing in this work are fictitious. Any resemblance to real persons, living or dead, is purely coincidental: Unless you are a self-aware alien computer trying to eke out a minor income living among the lesser humans by making and mending their primitive tools, then, yes, this book is probably inspired by your tale.

But, seriously, do not attempt any activities or experiments in this book or online without competent adult supervision. Science can be very dangerous.

Feedback and comments welcome – www.drjoe.id.au

To all those who are not easily offended – you are the salt of the earth. Everyone else, the savour that keeps life interesting; including bitterness, fake sweetness, and those sour, sour souls.

With much thanks to – Nathan Clark for teaching me how to use DAZ studio. To Samantha Ireland for believing in my dreams, and to each and everybody who read and edited this book – it belongs to you!

More wonderful titles by Dr Joe & Creating Science:

Delightful high fantasy for the thoughtful young reader

Choice, set free

1: The Quest of the Tae'anaryn

2: The Tae'anaryn and the Wizard's Apprentice

3: The Tae'anaryn and the Paladin's Squire

4: The Tae'anaryn and the Enchantress's Chrysalis

5: The Tae'anaryn and the Spear of the Troll Prince

6: The Tae'anaryn and the Khozmoh Djinn

An engaging science fiction adventure that introduces real science concepts to readers.

Space Chase 1: Arrendrallendriania

Space Chase 2: Elizabeth

Space Chase 3: Daniel

Space Chase 4: The Mechanizer

Thrilling young adult science fantasy adventure.

The Dragon Riders of Pearl

The Dragon Riders of Pearl 2: Seven Worlds

The Dragon Riders of Pearl 3: Return of the Plague

The Dragon Riders of Pearl 4: Rage of the Dragonmen

And for the budding scientist:

Creating Science – Dr Joe's book of science experiments and activities

Published by Creating Science by Dr Joe.

Table of contents

Table of images

Some important science concepts in the book:

It is a wildly ambitious project to weave simple yet profound science concepts within an engaging narrative, but we try. Here are a few science ideas that will help you get along, as well as who those ideas belong to as much as we can tell.

Inertia – by rolling marbles along ramps and using his formidable imagination, the 16th century Italian scientist Galileo Galilea came up with an idea that Isaac Newton would later coin as his rule of motion #1: That an object in motion will remain in motion unless acted upon by a force, and that an object at rest will remain at rest forever unless acted on by a force. This idea is now called Inertia.

Work – *work* has a special definition in science: it is defined as how far you can move an object, multiplied by how heavy the object is, in other words: mass times distance. If you move a 1 kilogram object 1 meter along, it has done 1 unit of work, measured in Joules (J). This simple idea, introduced in 1826 by the French mathematician Gaspard-Gustave Coriolis from his work with steam engines, is at the heart of almost all physics; moving something somewhere.

Acceleration – how much an object speeds up (or slows down). That is, its change in speed. DO NOT confuse acceleration with speed. Speed is how fast an object is moving. Acceleration is how fast or slow it changes that speed. Most physics deals with acceleration, not speed! (And as Einstein said, due to inertia all objects moving in a straight line at constant speed are entitled to consider themselves as not moving at all!)

Force – in science, a force is a push, a pull, or a twist. It is the power to make something move (i.e., it does "work".) Isaac Newton defined force very precisely, which allowed for much maths, as "an object's weight multiplied by its acceleration". He made this his law of motion #2.

This rule means, for instance, that a heavy (i.e., "massive") thing experiencing the same force as a light thing will speed up a lot less. So falling face first into the dirt places the same force on you and the Earth, but because the

Earth is so much more massive it decelerates a whole lot less than your face does.

Newton's law of motion #3 – in my opinion, the easiest and hardest law at the same time. Technically, "to every action there is an equal and opposite reaction." Practically, "all forces are in pairs", which means that if something gets pushed up, something else has to get pushed down. For example, if you want to swim left, what will you have to push right[1]? And if you want to jump up, you will have to push something down[2].

Friction – a special kind of force that turns motion into heat. It acts in the opposite direction of the motion to try and stop it. Without friction, it would be very hard to pick things up, brakes would not work and school students sitting on the floor would slide around like hockey pucks if you pushed them.

Traction – the amount of grip an object like a shoe or tyre has on the ground. It happens due to friction.

---

[1] The water, of course!

[2] The planet, obviously! Now according to Newton's Law #2, the earth is so much fatter (i.e., massive) that it 'wins' and it looks like you're the only one to move. But all forces, everywhere operate on different objects with an equal and opposite force. We have found no exception to this rule in the universe so far.

Chapter 1

How to kick a television

Chase looked down as the little TV robot tilted its TV head to one side, waiting for their answers, one of its squeaky, spindly feet digging in the soil impatiently.

And that was when Lucky, Chase's twin brother, decided that now was a good time to kick the TV robot in the head. It flew several meters and landed upside down in the bushes.

1 Lucky kicks the television

"Hey, what is your problem?!" Arren squealed at Lucky. Arren was Chase's best friend and she was an alien. Well, more of an alien spaceship with a humanoid robot she used to interact with people. A surprisingly-strong and maybe slightly-very-good-looking humaniform robot that had recently helped them start a school market, built a working hovercraft and travel with them to other dimensions. Arren had changed everything since she'd come along, but that was a long story. Short story was that she'd given Chase some very cool superpowers, like metalkinesis and telepathy, none of which seemed necessary to communicate with a little TV that had legs.

Lucky, however, *had* used his powers. Arren had given him superhuman strength and agility, and inhuman senses as well, none of which seemed to justify kicking a sentient robot into bushes. Perhaps it was the constant stream of assassin robots her "Dad" kept sending after them in an attempt to force her back home? They'd been dealing with the assassin robots over the past week and they'd ripped up the school tennis courts and upset the Australian Secret Service so much they'd almost kicked Arren off the planet. The attacks had set Chase so much on edge he'd almost torn the whole school apart by accident using a cyclone made of humanity's bad feelings. But that was all last week.

This week, there was a little TV robot with spindly legs hanging upside down in the bushes. It kicked its legs in a comically helpless attempt to right itself up.

Chase rushed over to help Arren set the little robot up again, which was a lot easier with his abilities and her strength.

"Just... mak'n sure you weren't another assassin," Lucky said, looking a little sorry.

Arren put the TV back on its feet and began to brush it down. "You all right, little fella?"

The robot brushed itself down indignantly. It had three mechanical legs and two spindly robot arms. The pixelated face that appeared on the square screen looked like a badly drawn image slapped on as a second thought. "Oh, indubitably. Your bodyguard is quite quick, I'll give him that."

"Bodyguard?" Lucky sounded unimpressed with the title, but Chase thought it quite accurate.

"You're a class 4?" Arren asked the robot. It seemed to be a designation living machines called each other by. Chase had his own class 3 – a little robot called Random. He was a shape shifter made of dust and a single crystal of quartz, and was currently pretending to be a very large wrist watch rather than looking for other robots to kick in the head. Random just liked to wait around until Chase needed him. Random was good value like that.

Arren was a class 2, or at least, her massive pyramid sized spaceship was. Arren was more like a person.

"Your designation is correct," the TV replied.

"What's the problem?" Arren asked. "What are you doing out here?"

"It's the Mechanizer," the little robot answered. "He's sick."

"Sick?" Chase asked. It didn't make much sense to him. The Mechanizer was another one of these alien robots hiding out on earth for various reasons. The Mechanizer was much less advanced, yet a whole lot older than Arren was. But they both were considered "alive", in a strange sort of way, with fears and things they loved, and if you asked any of them; a soul.

So maybe it wasn't completely strange that the Mechanizer could be ... sick.

"What do you mean?" Chase asked.

The TV robot looked down. "He took on too much. I don't think you guys know what's happening on this world, not really. Something went wrong. He broke, and now that's serious. We were working–"

"We?" Lucky asked. "Wait a minute, you work with the Mechanizer? Why haven't we met you before?"

The TV robot harrumphed, "I was right there the last time you visited. You mean you didn't even notice me?" He looked down, seeming sad. “Not that I should be surprised, no one ever does.”

“Aww, little guy. We’re noticing you,” Arren consoled the sentient robot. “What’s your name?”

“Ratchet,” he announced. “But that’s not my designation. Mechanizer never gave me one, now I think about it.” He dug his metal toe in the dirt and looked up and far away as though he was quite lost in that thought.

“You don’t need one,” Arren told him. “Come on, Ratchet, let’s get our bags home and then we’ll come–”

“If you please,” Ratchet interrupted, “I think this is far more serious than you realise. Perhaps it’s best if you see for yourself. Can we go there *immediately*?”

Arren looked concerned. Then she turned to Chase and his brother, “You boys up for an adventure?”

“Yup!” Chase agreed without hesitation.

“Sure...” Lucky replied with a reluctant sigh.

Within an instant they were inside Arren’s spaceship. She could make it teleport anywhere on earth – even to other star systems apparently. They had a quick sunbath, and the next instant they were deposited on the observation deck of the Mechanizer’s laboratory.

Chase had been here before, but it looked nothing like last time. It was immense, and it had grown. Thousands of gears and levers spun around on their own in a chaotic and purposeless fashion. Huge crank shafts and pinions floated through the air and Chase had to duck to avoid getting crushed.

The Mechanizer himself was at the far end of the room. At least, his face was; and either that was all he was or that was all they ever saw. It was made up of moving pieces of metal and machinery, but it looked very different to last time. Last time there was a kind of intelligent dignity to him. Now his mechanised face was… dirty. His metal pupils were constricted and his eyes unfocused. His voice, once wise and proud, was a muttering of meaningless syllables. And as Chase watched, it looked like another eye tried to form from the Mechanizer's cheek. Until he batted it away with machinery grabbed from the air.

"What's wrong?" Lucky shouted over the thunder of bouncing metal, busy building pointless devices and pulling them apart again.

"Not sure," Arren replied. She looked really worried. "It's as if he's trying to make something, or everything. He keeps pulling things apart for spare parts before he's finished whatever it is he's building. I've never seen anything like this. How long has this been going on?"

Ratchet replied, "He started going strange a few days ago, but it really took off this morning. I can't get through to him anymore, and I thought you might help." He sounded really worried, frightened even. He walked backwards and clutched on to the end of the platform with both his arm appendages. If TV's could gulp, it did.

Random jumped off Chase's wrist, and forming some kind of alien scanning device began beeping at the Mechanizer.

"Don't get too close!" Arren warned him. "I don't think he can tell friend from resource at the moment."

"Maybe he has a virus," Lucky suggested.

"A patent impossibility," Ratchet lectured, shaking a finger at Lucky. "Your planet's technology is vastly inferior, there is no way–"

Suddenly Arren squealed. It looked like some invisible force was pulling her off the platform.

Lucky was fast and grabbed her around the waist in a second. He tried to hold her down, but he was being pulled into the mess as well. Ratchet began throwing things and it seemed to distract the Mechanizer, who was still mindlessly trying to pull Arren towards him, presumably to rip her to pieces.

Arren's spaceship suddenly appeared in the air above their heads, but before it could do anything useful, the Mechanizer shouted with glee and began to rip it to shreds too. Arren screamed in pain – she was connected to her ship somehow and could feel it like her own body. Before Chase could save them, a few of the service spiders fell away and were torn to metal shreds.

"Chase!" Lucky screamed at him, "Help!"

Arren looked like she having trouble focusing through her pain. The Mechanizer suddenly dragged her and Lucky another meter toward the edge. Lucky jumped up and put his feet on the metal barrier, holding Arren away while standing sideways. It must have taken enormous strength.

"Arren, get us out of here!" Chase yelled.

It seemed to snap her out of her thoughts, and the spaceship vanished. The metal barrier Lucky was on began to bend, but Chase immediately strengthened it with his will.

Suddenly there was a squeal as Random flew right past him. With prescient instinct Chase reached out and grabbed him mid-air. Streams of dust still fell from the little satellite, but Chase pulled him in, still holding the metal barrier together.

But the Mechanizer was very determined. Two huge metal hands formed themselves from the chaos in the room, and Chase had to rip them to shreds with his mind.

Slowly, hand over hand, Arren and Lucky were edging themselves out of the Mechanizer's invisible reach. The end of the platform gave way as though torn apart by unseen jaws. Chase had to build another metal barrier using parts lying around, but it fell apart in seconds.

"Chase, the wall!" Arren shouted.

Chase immediately sensed that Arren had moved her teleporting spaceship outside the Mechanizer's wall. They needed to get out that way.

A moment later Random peeped a warning, and Chase turned around to see the Mechanizer was forming a haphazard, random collection of what looked like crossbows, except they were armed with oversized and overly sharpened screwdrivers.

Chase realised he could feel no pulling on him, apart from a slight tug on Random. He breathed out, trying to relax. Levitating was still a new thing to him, but it was one of the few superpowers Arren had not taught him – he was figuring it out for himself. It was tricky, and he'd found that the best way to do it was a little like walking – just do it, not think about it. Not be deliberate about it, just to step upwards and "forget to fall"[3]. He'd done it half a dozen times by accident, but never really deliberately, at least, not without oodles of concentration and plenty of time.

Random begged to help, but he knew if he let go the little robot would be torn to pieces.

Chase stepped off the platform, and for one heart stopping moment he felt himself begin to fall. But he fixed his mind and soul on watching the Mechanizer's face. He was determined to be too busy watching danger to remember to fall.

---

[3] Thank you, Hitch Hiker's Guide to the Galaxy.

It worked.

That challenge solved, Chase decided to fix the next two problems at once. With a wide wave of both his fists, he ripped the metal sheeting off the back wall, support struts and all. Somehow Arren and Lucky seemed to guess the plan and were already pinned to the floor.

Without knowing if he could, Chase strengthened the metal and held it out to cover Arren and Lucky. Not a moment too soon, for an instant later a hundred violent screwdrivers buried themselves in the makeshift shield.

He heard the Mechanizer mutter something. It sounded like, "Error repeats. What is the source of this unidentified obstacle? Orange pancake fickle breath," or something.

The strange metal eyes slowly turned in his direction, the pupils momentarily dilating to fix their gaze on him. In that instant, Chase recognised a strange, confused humanity in the mechanized being. He was a complete mess and it was pure torment to the poor living machine. Chase briefly wondered if he could, perhaps, reach that soul... perhaps... he could heal him.

"Obstacle located," the Mechanizer stated, eyes falling out of focus one more. "Remove immediately."

"Chase, we got to get out of here, now!" Arren shouted.

Chase floated up to join them as makeshift catapults formed at the far end of the room and began to throw metal orbs and bucket loads of steel axes at them. Chase saw

Arren's spaceship door, just outside the wall. It was glowing green, perhaps as a defence against the Mechanizer, or perhaps the broken machine simply couldn't reach outside his factory walls. Spears and axes began to fly their way, and Arren kicked one aside as Lucky somehow caught one. Ratchet vainly tried to reach up over the ledge and into Arren's ship but she was too busy trying to stop herself from getting pulled in to help.

So Chase floated himself into the green door. He then ripped up the entire metal floor where Lucky, Ratchet and Arren struggled along and used it to push them all into the spaceship and shield them a second time.

An instant later the air pressure altered so quickly there was a thundering boom and the entire factory disappeared. Lucky, Chase, Arren and Ratchet were all inside her spaceship, somewhere over a dark ocean at night time. He checked them all out to see if everyone was safe.

"We all here?" Lucky shouted, looking around desperately.

Chase looked at Lucky, disentangling himself from Arren's hair. He saw Ratchet trembling in her arms. Then he opened his hand to find a clear quartz crystal that was Random's inner computer. A few flecks of black dust still clung to his outer shell, but he was all right.

"All present and accounted for," Chase replied with a relieved smile.

Chapter 2

But that was another time

(Several days before chapter 1)

Chase had to admit that getting dragged along the school oval at the end of a rope was one of the least pleasant experiences he had ever had. The dirt got everywhere – in his nose, in his shorts, in his eyes. The resulting burn he got from the excessive rubbing of his torso as it was dragged though the dust itched for the rest of the day[4].

Trust school to not be cancelled just because someone put a few holes in it and knocked down the school hall, Lucky had protested.

It was Wednesday, a few days before the issue with the Mechanizer had kicked in. They were on the school oval doing science as a class, and because the school hall still wasn't fixed yet so they had to do science in one of the undercover areas.

At one end of the rope was Lucky and Chase, and at the other end was Mark T, the classic school bully, and one of his lackeys. They were calling themselves the 'Intraplanetary Defence Force' now, since Mark had figured

---

[4] This is often called 'carpet burn' and is caused by excessive friction.

out that Arren was an alien. He was even posting about it on social media, which it seemed everyone thankfully ignored. Mark T was smart, but sort of evil. He'd shoved Chase to the ground at least once a year since grade 2 and it looked like today was the special event for year 9.

Their science teacher had decided to teach them about forces and motion, and with the abundance of outside space teachers had to work with right now, he seemed to have decided a tug-of-war was the way to do it.

"I'm going to kick his butt," Lucky had said.

"I don't think we should use our powers," Chase had disagreed.

"Speak for yourself, mind-boy," Lucky argued. "I can't ***not*** use my strength. What, am I supposed to turn off my muscles?"

"It doesn't work like that," Chase had said. He was already fighting back a misgiving. It was two against two; it should be a fair fight. He was trying not to read Mark T's very disturbed mind, but he was already looking a little too confident.

"Aaaaand, go!" the teacher had shouted.

Mark T was the anchor man for his team, and Chase for theirs. Mark T immediately lent so far backwards he almost fell over, his body ridged and tense.

Lucky, however, stood up very tall and yanked with all his super human strength. The rope probably should have snapped, but it was one of those stupidly heavy ropes made for tug of war that you couldn't do anything stupid like twist around your limb or something[5].

For reasons Chase could not explain, Lucky's sudden tug didn't seem to pull Mark T and his lackey towards them, but rather, pulled Chase and Lucky right off their feet and towards Mark T. They flew several meters in the air, making it look for all purposes as though Mark T had the super human strength and not Lucky. With savage glee Mark T and lackey pulled him and his brother another meter or two through the dirt before Lucky realised what was happening, and with an athletic twist dug his heals into the dirt and stood up.

And as his mouth and eyes filled with soil, Chase managed a kind of telepathic peek at Mark T, and immediately saw the problem. The fat bully was cheating again. He had somehow managed to bring along some soccer boots with some unusually long spikes in the sole of his shoe. They looked like nails. Actually, they *were* nails. Some of them were 10 centimetres long!

---

[5] Because someone actually did that, once. The combined force of a hundred people pulling a rope in opposite directions can truly be enormous. Don't wrap your limbs around any rope about to be pulled taught or it may also get torn off.

BTW, can your class pull harder than an elephant?

This explained why Mark wasn't moving – his super long spikey shoes were dug into the soil, granting him some impressive resistance to being moved. That, and Chase had to admit he was a pretty tough kid. Lucky's sudden yank had almost dislocated both of Mark's shoulders, but he hung in there with the very best of human determination Chase had ever seen. It was kind of impressive.

Lucky, on the other hand, was already standing on his tip toes at the very edge of the line. Tip toes, versus ten centimetre nails dug into the soil. Lucky was, miraculously, pulling with a force sufficient to match Mark T and his buddy – at least without pulling himself over again. They were completely, evenly, matched.

Chase realised he could tip that balance, but yanking on the rope might make Lucky loose his footing. Then again, Mark T had been cheating. Chase realised he could psychokinetically bend the nails at his feet or try some regular telekinesis. Although, he didn't seem very good at it. Maybe he could convince Mark T to let go, but Chase hadn't tried controlling other people's minds yet.

And in the moment of indecision, Mark T pushed with all his might into the soil and pulled Lucky over the line. They cheered and pumped the air.

"Ha! Losers, again!" Mark T shouted.

"Hey!" The teacher called. It seemed the teachers were also getting sick of the bulling.

Lucky turned and helped Chase up, looking confused. "How'd we lose buddy?"

"Mark T has nails thiiiis long under his shoes," Chase explained.

"That cheater!" Lucky clenched a fist. "First, he hits me in the head with a crowbar, then he has to beat us both at tug-of-war? I'm telling the teacher."

"Don't. How will you explain how you know?" Arren said, coming up with the others. Including Kassie, her other new best friend Chase and Lucky had still never talked to.

Lucky muttered to himself under his breath.

"I still don't get how we lost." Chase asked Arren. She was an expert at science and technology. They were talking about having her compete in the regional robotics challenge for the school, which wouldn't really have been very fair on everyone else – Arren *was* a robot.

"Well, it all has to do with the nature of a force," Arren explained. "Forces are a push, a pull, or a twist if you ask some experts. But as Isaac Newton explained with rule number three – 'to every action there is an equal and opposite reaction' ".

"Yes, I've heard that," Chase answered. "But what does it mean?"

"It means," Arren explained, helping knot Kassie's hair back into a plait, because that was what was apparently happening right now. "It means 'forces are always in pairs.

Equal in power, but opposite in direction, and acting on two different objects'. You know what I mean? When you want to swim left, you have to push the water to the right. That force of your push will push you left, but the water will also experience the force and it will move right. Got that? So what if you want to go up?"

"I guess I'll have to push something down, like the ground?"

"Spot on!" she complimented him. "Except the ground is so much bigger that it wins. That's rule number 2. Now back to the rope. When Lucky gave a super-tug on the rope, the force went both ways. On him, and on Mark T. So the force was pulling you both together."

"And because Mark T had ten centimetre nails stuck into the ground, he 'won', and Lucky and I were the only ones that moved."

"Right," Arren admitted. "Tug of war is really a contest of who has the most traction on the ground. The force between them is the same. Kinda ironic really. The Roman army had tug-of-war contests all the time. They pulled a lot of ropes, you see; moving siege engines and sailing triremes and such. Strange, isn't it? To pull someone towards you, you have to brace yourself against your own force by pushing on the ground in the opposite direction as you're pulling."

"Weird," Lucky said.

Kassie wasn't saying anything, Chase wasn't sure she was even listening.

"It's like this!" Arren said, getting excited and running over to the undercover area. She sat down on the teacher's wheeled chair without asking and grabbed the teacher's desk. "Try this, Chase. Look, if I sit next to the table and pull on the table, who's going to move, me or the table?"

"The table, of course," Kassie said.

"No," Chase disagreed. Apparently he'd been in the same class as Kassie since kindergarten but he could not remember it. "The chair has no traction. Arren's pull will only make her move."

"Seriously?" Kassie said, clearly not believing him.

Arren gave a long tug, and her chair rolled predicably into the table.

"No waaaaay!" Kassie shouted. She ran over and shoved Arren out of the chair. Chase guessed they liked each other. They seemed to make each other laugh a lot. Kassie pulled herself into the table, then out again. Then in, then out. "Ka-booooom," she whispered, indicating that Arren had blown her mind again.

Arren laughed. How predicable. She put her hands on Kassie's shoulders and stopped her from moving forwards. The traction seemed enough, and with some forceful yanking Kassie slowly slid the table towards her while yelling frantically.

It was quite comical. Even the teacher was laughing.

"I did not know that about tug-of-war," Lucky admitted, looking at the girls side on as if he thought they might both actually be aliens.

Chapter 3
Shakedown

(2 seconds after chapter 1 ended)

Back on the spaceship, Arren shoved Lucky off her and started rubbing her feet furiously.

"Well, what happened?" Lucky asked.

Random spoke using telepathy to convey his thoughts to their minds. He seemed to prefer communicating that way. *I believe the Mechanizer has contracted a deleterious morphing algorithm. It could not have originated from Earth.*

Chase sat back down and breathed a sigh of relief. "What's a delete-rious... morphy... one of those things!"

"It's a virus," Arren announced. She tried to stand, but fell right over again.

Chase helped pick her up.

"That guy is nuts. He almost killed me Chase!" She looked in his eyes, as if to see how he would react.

Chase didn't know how to react. Was she stating facts? Or looking for sympathy?

A service spider arrived and she sat down on it. "I need to visit the medical room. Coming?"

"Might as well," Chase replied, and was a little surprised when she hauled him up on the spider as well. Lucky and

Ratchet walked along behind, but Arren kicked off her shoes and made Chase rub her feet while she clutched on to him, clearly uncomfortable. "This is a serious situation, guys. A very serious situation. Ouch, ow, ow, ow!"

"You all right, Arren?" Lucky asked. It seemed a ridiculously obvious question.

It was little wonder Arren was unimpressed. "No I am NOT all right, Lucky! That madman ripped off half my ankle and two toes! Oh, and I lost Nor Driarnia and Tzallen! That little guy's been with me right from the beginning. Ouch! Someone's going to pay for that. Oh, ow, ouch, ouch!"

"You're welcome for saving your life," Lucky muttered.

She signed, "Thank you for saving my life, Lucky. And Chase. We really should have looked into it more. Didn't either of you humans have a psychic warning? A misgiving? Nothing set off your spider sense?"

Everyone looked at him. "Ahh," Chase said. He didn't have an answer for that either.

"Whatever, lay off him," Lucky said. "We going to let the authorities know?"

"They're on their way. Or, rather, we're on our way once we know they're ready to meet us. All of us. We've got a serious situation here boys. This one's already well out of my field of expertise."

***

Twelve people sat around the polished eucalyptus wood table. They were probably high ranking spies and agents for the Australian Security and Intelligence Organisation. They all wore ties and business suits including, as fate would have it, the woman in charge – Lucky and Chase's mother, Elizabeth. She wore a classy lady business suit with a formal pink and grey lady-tie. She looked good, and quite a bit younger than she actually was. Chase hadn't seen her since he tried to apologise for busting up the school and almost levelling the suburb last week, so he was glad to see she was up and herself again. That meant she was all business, didn't trade any pleasantries, and insisted they call her "Elizabeth" or "Ms Grey" in all professional decisions – anything other than "Mum".

But Chase couldn't stop himself smiling to see her.

She nodded at them as soon as they teleported into the room, the closest thing he could expect to a hug. Predictably, that was as far as her socialising went. "Arren, we have not all had time to read your hastily written report. I question your wisdom at sending a memo to the American embassy without involving us first."

Arren replied quickly, walking to the foot of the table so that she could see and be seen by all the people there. "Earth does not have a current planetary government, but they do have a dominating planetary culture – and for the time being that is the Americans. Telling them is the quickest way to let the whole world know, because I guarantee you, your planet has less than 2 days to resolve this problem or it won't matter who the dominating culture is in the coming techno-apocalypse."

"What do you mean?" a man asked. He was fairly old, quite well dressed, and spoke with a polished British accent. He was sitting next to mum, across from the two most annoying spies Chase had ever met – officers Costa and Flannigan. He hoped he would have nothing to do with them right now.

2 Coast, Elizabeth, and Flannigan

Arren answered, and as she did, Random popped down and formed himself into a mini, but ridiculously bright, 3D hologram projector. Whatever Arren wanted to say was immediately projected into the centre of the room.

"The Mechanizer has been infected by a deleterious morphing algorithm, a 'virus', for want of a better word." Images of the computer program appeared in the air, displaying the algorithm's complex interdimensional programming. It looked perverse; a twisting, morphing, spiked worm that lashed out aggressively at the dancing sheets of energy around it, tearing and reorganising them in chaotic fashions. It *looked* evil. "It would have been implanted around 5 days ago, creating exponential cascade failure in the Mechanizer."

"What does that mean for us?" the man asked.

"As near as I can figure out, the Mechanizer holds to his original desire to reorganise and create, though he no longer has the ability to hold a coherent thought or recognise friend from resource. He will not stay within his initial safety protocols in any way."

"Meaning?" Mum asked.

Arren held up her hands, it seemed that while this had to be told, Arren did not want to say it. "Meaning, he will create whatever random aberration appears in his imagination. The vast majority of which will be harmless, but he may also create actually dangerous things –

mechanised monsters, weapons, and God help us – Von Neumann machines[6]."

"Von Neumann? Sounds human," the man said.

"A Hungarian born mathematician," Mum replied. "He developed the theory of infinitely self-replicating machines."

Arren looked grim, "More like giant, super advanced, chaos machines in our case."

"How many?" he asked.

"How... did you not..." Arren was getting flustered. "The Mechanizer has ***no limits*** at the moment. He cannot recognise friend from foe, or nature from resource. He will not stop until this entire world is one purposeless machine right to the core, and then he'll cyber-form the moon and every other planetary object in your solar system. Then, if we're lucky, he'll either stop or the Unity will step in."

"The Universal Unity," the man said with a grim smile. "One of the least helpful organisations in existence."

"They're not so bad," Arren replied with sarcasm, "Once you stop enslaving your own race and destroying all your natural resources."

The man huffed. Chase had to agree, world peace was still a ways off for now.

---

[6] From https://en.wikipedia.org/wiki/Self-replicating_machine - while they're a great idea for colonising space, they're also a great idea for bringing about the end of the world (see 'Grey Goo').

"Looks like we're on our own again," the spy named Flannigan grinned. He was always grinning. Like he knew something no one else did or he was simply didn't care. He might have been insane. That was Chases' favourite theory. But Lucky liked him, or was at least willing to get along with him. Flannigan was wearing casual clothes and his blond hair was a mess as though someone had just pulled him off holidays for the meeting. Chase wished he could tell more of what they were thinking now that he had some reasonably well developed mind reading powers, but they'd gotten wise to him and blocked him somehow. Not that it mattered, right now stopping a sick robot from destroying the world in two days was the priority. How were they supposed to do that?

"So how are we supposed to stop a messed up machine from destroying the world in only two days?" Lucky asked.

"I take it you had no luck," Mum said.

"Disastrous," Arren replied. "I can't get anywhere near him from any of my usual or unusual routes. He's gone insane."

"Direct assault?" Flannigan suggested. "We can have the international forces there in under six hours, have him shut down the hard way."

"Unadvisable." Ratchet suddenly peeped up. No one seemed to question his presence, and Chase wondered if they'd already met him somewhere. He was an old buddy of the Mechanizer after all, and the Mechanizer was generally a very helpful fellow, or he used to be. "For now, he seems to consider humans non-resources, but I cannot say how long that will hold out."

"Humans?" Mum asked.

"Yes, humans," Arren replied. "Your bones are mostly calcium and your blood is rich in iron. You'd make wonderful resources to a mortally ill machine bent of self-preservation. Also–"

"Nuclear assault," Costa stated flatly. He was the other secret service agent assigned to Arren's case, and he was sitting bolt upright and still wearing a suit like he did every time, as though he didn't own any other clothes. He was a humourless devotee, so Chase understood him even if he didn't agree with him. At least they were on the same team right now. Costa had tried to kill the last thing that stood in his way. Come to think of it, shooting things seemed to be Costa's default way of dealing with problems. "Have the American's use one of their secret orbital warheads."

Arren sighed, "They're moving one into position now. But I advise against it. The Mechanizer is too advanced. He will work out it's a weapon as soon as you lock on – before it is even fired. As soon as it's in range he'll tear it to pieces and use its weapon grade uranium to build more machines. Besides, there's one other problem."

"And?" the older man asked in her silence.

"And, for now, the Mechanizer is not on self-defence mode. Once you start attacking you're going to activate his protective algorithms, which will immediately be infected by the virus, if they aren't already. If he isn't building advanced weapons by now, he will be about one second after you attack him. If he cannot yet tell friend from foe, or even self from others, he will definitely create the worst kinds of disasters in self-defence. I can't imagine – earthquakes, self-aware guided missiles. It's like I said, you have a very serious situation here."

"Then what would you have us do?" Elizabeth asked.

"We don't have a lot of options," Arren admitted with a sigh. "If you do attack, hold nothing back. Scorch the earth, if you have to. Consider him a primal elemental evil, an eldritch abomination. There's always a chance his condition will worsen to the point of self-destruction, and the self-defence protocols are designed to hasten that in any species[7]. A long term war of attrition may go on for decades, but that's our last option. I'm going to go to Negkletheule on your behalf. They have some of the best programmers in any of the near galaxies, and anyone wanting the continued

---

[7] An interesting claim by Arren, but the parallel in biological species is clear. The 'fight or flight' response of dire self-defence, which gives us the adrenaline rush, reduces pain response and much more, yet it is only designed as a short term state. When kept up for too long it results in fatigue, exhaustion, and potentially death.

support of the Unity needs to show kindness – I think they will help us."

"There is another option," the old man with the British accent stated. When it was clear no one was going to interrupt, he continued. "You need to see the Caretaker."

Arren looked grim. "Even if I knew how, he hasn't attempted to contact me. Besides," she turned to Chase to encourage him to speak.

"Besides," Chase replied. "One of the class 2 probes that was sending in the assassin robots from a nearby earth dimension told me that he was here on the invitation of this, 'Caretaker.' I, for one, would very much like to know who he is, and why he did that."

The man sighed, and looked around the room. "There's a lot we don't know about this individual, and would very much rather hope that you could shed some more information on who he is for us."

Mum took her chance to speak up to explain to some of the other confused looks at the table. "Since the recent situation involving the assassin robots, it turns out that there is yet another alien entity on our world. An enigmatic individual known only as the Caretaker. He seems to have taken it upon himself for quite some time now to decide which alien life forms have his permission to visit and indeed, stay, on Earth."

"Given that it's not even his decision to make, it is a curious claim at best," Costa argued with a fist. "Who does he think he is?"

"At any rate," the British man said, "I'm afraid you know all the intel we possess at this point in time. But I believe that anyone with the ability to keep the entire Coebri space pirate trading conglomerate off our world might have the ability to deal with the situation we currently face. We may simply have to find the Caretaker."

Arren looked serious. "I thought the Unity kept my father's empire away from planet earth?"

"We simply assumed the Caretaker worked for them," the man admitted. "Now, I'm not so sure."

"What if your plan with the Negkletheule fails?" said Mum, her pronunciation of that weird planet's name truly excellent. "Are we really reduced to the hard way?"

"There is... another way. You can't be expected to deal with this threat. It would take a dozen years and cost millions of human lives. If I went nuclear and came down from orbit, I could take him out. Death toll – only two, apart from a minor orbital shift and a decimating climate change."

"Not ideal," Mum replied. "I like the climate. Also, the Mechanizer is too useful. We would be disappointed to lose him. Also, Arren..." she said nothing more, seeming to imply with her silence that she did not like this idea of Arren sacrificing herself for more personal reasons. Perhaps she was learning to like Chases's new space friend?

Chase also did not want Arren to die, but could see it had to be a better idea than a decade of war with chaos machines. "Can we come up with a plan C, first?" he asked.

"D," Flannigan replied.

"C," Arren persisted. "Scorched earth is everyone's last resort. It's plan Z. A, we get help from Negkletheule. B, find the Caretaker and get answers. D, Arren blows herself up by an orbital bombardment resulting in a smoking crater almost a kilometre deep and a decade of global winter no one is prepared for. C... I don't have a plan C. Let me know if you can come up with one."

"Can't we just hack in," Flannigan asked, "Shut him down remotely?"

Arren almost laughed, "That's plan B. You think you got the tech to do it? Your entire internet combined is an insignificant amount of data compared to the Mechanizer. Every human on earth would need a million years each just to scan through his memory and you still wouldn't know what you were looking for. No, this is out of your reach. It's out of mine. We go to Negkletheule or we bunker down for either a decade of winter or a decade of war."

"Let's see what we can do." Mum said, "Flannigan, get on the programmers. See what they can turn out, and keep the public blind. You know the drill. Costa, get onto military worldwide. Give them all we know and get to ground zero ASAP. Make sure Honk Kong is fully briefed on what's going on. Governor," she said turning to the old man who had done a lot of talking, "We need intel on the Caretaker, would you mind seeing what you can bring in?"

He sighed, "I can only try. You're still better equipped at this than I."

"Unlikely," she disagreed. "Arren – "

"Get to Negkletheule!" Arren finished for her. "And, if you don't mind too much, I'd like to take Lucky and Chase with me. For the adventure, you know."

For just a moment mum looked concerned, like she cared. It was nice. "Very well then, but bring my sons back in one piece, all right?"

"Always," Arren said. "But, if you don't mind, I'll need some cream cheese."

Mum looked surprised. "Sure, just use the government account."

"I have my own funds, thank you!" Arren said, and as Random hopped back on to Chase's wrist, the entire room disappeared, and was replaced a moment later by a dark alley.

"You're getting better at this!" Lucky complimented her new found accuracy at teleporting.

"They're letting me use the GPS satellites now." Arren explained. "In return for calibrating them occasionally. It's a hobby. But it was pretty annoying not being able to use them since all they do is beep and it's pretty hard to ignore that from the surface of the earth[8]!'

They followed her, walking toward a well-lit street. Chase soon recognised it as the local shops.

Arren wasn't hurrying, but she was moving pretty quick. Making sure no one was watching, she teleported into the store, grabbed the cheese, teleported to the registers, bought the cheese and jogged out. "Ready?"

"Oooh, another space adventure!" Lucky grinned.

"It'll take us 4 minutes to get there and another half hour or so to get down from orbit. We need to be polite, but I'm hoping they'll speed it up for us."

"You going to make us wear costumes again?" Lucky moaned.

"We are on a diplomatic mission to save your world, Lucky. I'm just glad they didn't insist on sending any of their own overly cautious and under-trained 'interspecies diplomats'. Come on, boys," she said, turning down the alley as her ship materialised around them. "Let's go save planet Earth!"

---

[8] Did you know that's how the GPS satellites work? It's worth looking into. Basically, the satellites don't tell your phone where it is. The satellites just 'beep', and your phone decides where it must be on earth by listening to the beeps.

Chapter 4

The planet with a name that's really hard to pronounce

Now they stood in front of a massive prismatic force field. It looked thin, like moving glass, and behind it an empty room was vaguely visible.

"Should I knock?" Chase asked.

"I wouldn't. That's an interforce redundancy field. At low levels it absorbs your force completely so that no one will hear you knocking on the other side."

"And at higher levels?" Lucky asked.

"It generates the hypothetical monoforce[9] and applies the *entire* force back at you. I know that doesn't make sense. You just have to believe me."

"So we wait?" Chase wondered.

"She'll know we're here," Arren said.

They waited a moment.

---

[9] I made this up. As far as we know, there are NO single forces in nature: Always equal and opposite. However, science fiction almost always has forces acting in one direction and not two, which is *bad sci-fi!* Unless, of course, they admit it's a made up thing, like I'm doing. That's good sci-fi. Good sci-fi, yes you are, yes you are!

"Well, I liked the Negkletheulians," Lucky announced. "No fuss, no welcoming rituals apart from a brief 'greetings'. Got right to business, didn't they?"

"I guess they liked that cheese," Chase said.

"They know it's an emergency," Arren told him.

There was a pause. Then Lucky spoke again, "And apparently their local expert does not, or she does not care. Why is she keeping us waiting?"

"Because maybe she's doing something important?" Arren argued.

"I'm gonna knock," Lucky told them.

"That's not a good idea," Chase argued. He had no idea what an interforce redundancy field was capable of.

"We don't have time. We're standing here, wasting five minutes."

"Actually, it's more like six," Arren announced.

"Felt like five," Lucky muttered.

"It was," Arren replied, making little sense.

They looked at her.

"OK, five to us, six to most of the rest of the universe."

"How do you go figure?"

"Sometimes you boys worry me. The Coebri kids learn this in kindergarten. Time dilation, guys. Did any of you notice them tell us their local expert had shifted focus and was now studying black holes?"

"I remember something about a singularity[10]," Lucky said.

"Oh, yeah," Chase remembered. "A black hole."

Lucky gasped, "We're IN a black hole!"

"No we are not IN a black hole Lucky!" Arren seemed to be losing her temper. "We're NEXT to one. A big one. And did you know, and I know you do not, that where gravity gets strong, time slows down[11]? I'm sure I've mentioned this to you somewhere. So, near the edge of this black hole on this stationary research platform, time is moving slower than in the rest of the universe."

"I don't want to be one minute in the past when we get home!" Lucky shouted.

---

[10] Named after the mathematical principal when an equation reaches an infinite value. For example, the equations for black holes have infinite density. Since we don't have any maths or science to explain what happens at that point, we're not really sure what happens inside black holes. But they are sometimes called 'singularities'.

[11] To be precise, time slows down using the equation:

Gravitational time dilation on the Earth's surface:

$$T = \frac{T_0}{\sqrt{1 - \frac{2gR}{c^2}}}$$

Where g = force of gravity, R = distance between the centre of the objects and c= the speed of light. To find the time dilation here on the earth; g = 9.8 m/s2 (force of gravity on earth), R = 6.38 x 106m (mean radius of Earth), and c= 3 x 108m/s (speed of light in a vacuum).

"It doesn't work like that, thankfully," Arren explained, rubbing her brow in frustration. "They'll be one minute older than you, but you're not in the past or anything."

"That's it. I'm not waiting another minute." And with that he underarm punched the force field with all his might.

It was just like the tug of war. With almost no traction on the floor, all that force went right back into Lucky and threw him across the room. It probably should have broken some bones, but miraculously didn't.

"Ouch," Lucky muttered.

"Ouch," Arren agreed.

"Cool," Chase grinned at his brother – ever willing to test the laws of physics and prove Arren right again.

"You'd have as much luck punching the earth out of orbit as you would have punching this barrier in, Lucky. It's not that it's too heavy; it has no mass at all actually. But it experiences no force on itself while returning all the force back at you. A paradoxical monoforce that ends up giving you twice the force you originally applied. I don't think she even heard–"

Suddenly the force field dissolved.

"Who's that making all this racket out here?!" An ornery voice complained. It was another Negkletheulian – short and stout, with messy hair and odd jewellery all over her scaly, dark skinned neck. Chase thought she spoke very good English. "We're trying to research in here, don't you know!"

"Excuse us," Arren apologised, making the appropriate gestures of peace and supplication. "We are from–"

"Earth. Yes, I can tell from the *smell*. You're not supposed to be out here. Your civilisation is barely nuclear and now you're trying to get a cut of my leading-edge research into the primal force of the fundamental four[12]?"

Arren looked confused and turned to Chase, probably hoping his intuition would somehow know what to say.

"Please," he began, feeling nervous. This Negkletheulian was not like the other more organised sorts. She looked upset. "Please, there's a situation on Earth."

"What do I care?!" The Negkletheulian shouted, turning away. "Burn that cesspool to the ground, I say!"

"Now that's not very polite," Arren protested.

She turned back again. "No one said a Coebri was coming today as well. Thieves. Come to look at my research have you?"

---

[12] In physics, we are aware of four fundamental forces in nature: gravity, electromagnetism (which makes electricity and magnetism, and holds different atoms together), the weak nuclear force (that moderates how atoms decay), and the strong nuclear force (that holds the nucleuses of atoms together despite being made up of only neutral or positive charges). Of these fundamental forces we know the least about gravity, but if you really look at the situation we still have a lot to learn about all the fundamental forces of the universe!

Arren looked offended, "You've not got anything I don't already know," she replied, probably unwisely.

The Negkletheulian huffed and popped her cheeks, looking too upset to talk. It was really beginning to look like the entire discussion was about to fall apart.

Then Lucky spoke. "Listen, shorty," he said, rubbing his fist from the floor. "We got a mad robot about to destroy our planet and every living thing on it, and they said you were the one who could help. So, are you going to help, or what?"

Chase held his breath. After attempting to bash in her front door, he couldn't imagine a ruder thing to say.

To his surprise, the Negkletheulian nodded her head and waved them in, "Very well, humans of earth, and your Coebri pilot. Right this way."

Lucky looked very smug as he walked past Arren, who looked like she didn't know whether to hug him or slap him. Thankfully, she did neither.

Passing through the doorway felt amazing, and very difficult to explain. It felt like gravity all twisted for a moment. His leading hand and foot were moving faster than they should, and after his head was through, his trailing hand and foot seemed to get a little stuck in the space behind the force field. It was amazing to feel what rapid time compression felt like.

"They got those in every Coebri school playground," Arren told him.

He shook his head, wishing he could have one of his own to experiment with.

The room beyond was a very neatly organised research facility, and his jaw hit the floor[13] when he saw the view outside the main window – indescribable. He had no idea just how close they were to the black hole when Arren had teleported them here.

A massive blue star was clearly visible in iridescent glory, streams of burning plasma trailing off it and into a dark orb so small it could barely be seen, a deep crimson disc where a dying sun met the feasting black hole. Two bright streams of white energy blasted off the top and bottom of the black hole, flying out into the immensity of space infinitely in two directions. To see a super massive star this close was truly impressive, but to see it effortlessly ripped apart by something so small it could barely be seen was even more amazing.

Arren tried to say something, but the Negkletheulian waved her to silence so that he could enjoy the scene a moment more.

---

[13] One of the silliest terms of expression our culture has ever come up with. I can't stand it. But "he opened his mouth in surprise," just doesn't seem to convey the same meaning...

"Impressed, are you, Earth-boy? This is but a little wonder that your universe has to offer you. Have you seen the sun-engulfing cities of the Coebri yet? The ultra-dimensional worlds of the Unity? No wonder I'm the only physical observer of this minor work of art at the moment."

3 A feasting black hole. Courtesy of NASA

She walked off, holographic screens springing to life around her as she moved, twisted, and programmed them all without looking. "You want to see something beautiful? You should see the maths we use to describe that thing."

"I would like to see that."

She looked sorry for him, "Wish I could show you, but Unity got rules against that sort of thing."

"What are you working on?" Lucky asked.

"Te, he," she laughed. "Meathead still got his brain in? That's good. But still, lucky you don't read Negkletheulian or I'd be in real trouble. Maths... my oldest friend. You need some heavy reprogramming if you're going to take on a class 3 Coebri Reclamation vessel; especially if he's got what I suspect he's got. I'll need a few hairs."

"Will mine do?" Lucky offered.

"NO!" She shouted. "It's a figure of speech! What do you use, I need some *time*." [14]

"Oh," Lucky said.

She grinned at him, like she actually cared about him. She bent her head and kept working.

Arren stared at the screens.

Lucky pressed his hands up against the windows, and it rippled underneath his fingers like the door did. At first he pulled back, naturally mistaking it for some kind of water. "At least we'll be safe here. Wonder how long she'll be?"

Apparently, more than an hour. Arren tried to help but the Negkletheulian kept shutting her down and disagreeing.

---

[14] Thank goodness we don't use this phrase, 'I need a few hairs'. But sayings are often this strange, though they often once made clear sense when they first came into common usage.

Finally, the old woman swept all the holographic windows she was working on into a small, marble sized glass orb.

"Nice marble," Lucky said.

She looked annoyed again, "This ... child's toy is exactly what you need. Just bring it to within several meters of your rogue class 3, and it'll do the rest."

"Thank you," Chase said.

"Thank you!" Arren beamed, making the appropriate gestures of gratitude and thanks.

"Well," the old scientist said, "at least this one knows how to show some gratitude! Here, give us a hug, human."

Arren interposed herself between them in an instant. "That's hardly fair," she protested for some unknown reason.

The Negkletheulian grinned sheepishly. "All right then, a handshake. How often does one get to shake the hand of an Earther still under the veil? Not often. Here, good boy. And you, meat head. Show some gratitude!"

She held out her hand expectantly. Chase checked with Arren who was watching the handshake like some kind of hawk or a judge watching a trial. He didn't know what it was about, so he carefully stretched out his hand to shake hers.

The moment she took it there was a stifling riot of visions that flashed past his mind. He seemed to see every aspect of the scientists past, present, and future self, stretching on in an inexplicably infinite line in both directions. It momentarily stunned him.

"Oh, this one is beginning to get the hang of it," she said, letting go.

It took him a moment to refocus.

"Welcome to normal," she said, seeming to refer to the visions, and not drawing away from them.

"How did you do that?" Chase asked.

She looked puzzled, but never did explain. She went then to shake Lucky's hand, and he looked a little subdued but didn't seem to have any visions or anything.

"Classic meat head," the old scientist said, and patted him on the cheek. "I like you."

Lucky smiled.

She then held out the little marble, and Lucky held out his hand to have her drop it in. Then the scientist gasped, and closed her fist around the marble.

Suddenly Arren gasped and faced the front door.

Then there was a thunderous explosion from outside.

A coarse, hate filled voice filled the room from somewhere. "Surrender the class 2 in the name of Lord Tzaark of the Coebri, or suffer the consequences!" it roared.

Chase snarled. It looked like Arren's dad was back in town...

Chapter 5

Blood is thicker than quark-gluon plasma

"Coebri!" the old scientist shouted angrily. Chase could feel the air begin to sizzle around her. She shouted at whoever had blasted her front porch. "Respect your treaty with the Negkletheule and the Unity! Be gone!"

"Well," a snide voice replied, "We're not exactly in Negkletheule space right now, are we?"

The old scientist gasped, "You wouldn't dare!"

"Just hand over the unit Arren Drallen Driarnia and nobody will get hurt!"

Arren looked worried. She looked like she was about to say something like, 'Let me talk to them,' though she could have said, 'I don't belong to Negkletheule either. Why are you trying to make them hand me over?' but she never got either chance…

…Because the entire front door exploded.

Chase briefly wondered how they managed that with a monoforce, but decided it wasn't worth it.

Nobody moved.

"C'mon boys. It's me they want," Arren said.

"They blew in my front door!" the scientist muttered. "So, they want to see how we Negkletheulian scientists deal with unwelcomed guests do they?" She strode forward, manifesting a glowing green staff right into her hands without any apparent effort.

Arren skipped in behind her, and simply because it was convenient Chase stood on her left, Lucky at her right. Lucky looked excited and angry.

They strode out on to a devastated balcony which used to be the welcoming room. Outside the gaping hole some kind of glowing green force field was protecting the space station from the black hole, the glowing accretion disc so bright it could have blinded him. But the field had been shredded in at least two places, covered with red Coebri force fields patching the holes they'd torn there. It looked very dangerous, and just a little precarious.

Four small Coebri fighter craft, designed for two each, hovered threateningly in the air. And behind them, two massive vessels patched the holes in the force field. They were strange alien vessels, with mismatched units attached together without any real planning for final form. They had weird cranes and pullies, exhaust pipes and ladders all over them. One was shaped like football, the other a tilted cube – a rhombus. They looked oddly familiar, but Chase could not quite figure out where he'd seen them before. They almost looked like...

"More 'Arrens'..." Lucky muttered.

And that was when Chase realised what they were. Just like Arren's pyramid spaceship. They were two highly advanced Research and Reclamation vessels. They were other 'Arrens'.

Three figures stood on the ground before Chase and his friends. The first was an old man in a white robe. He looked nervous and was caked with dust. Behind him there was another human man. He was dirty and armed with a strange rifle and what might have been several glowing grenades on his chest. Right behind him, clinging to his pants and with eyes wide open was a little six year old girl.

"Well, well, well," the armed man gloated. " 'Ere's a sight for sore eyes – Arren, pride of me Master's soul! What are you doing 'ere child? Yer making yer father ill with worry."

Arren simmered with anger, but the old scientist wouldn't let her pass. Arren seemed to calm down, "Always a liar, aren't you, First? How will you report your failure to return me to slavery again?"

He looked angry, but it was the old man who interrupted, "Arrendrallendriania," he said with bowed head and forced smile. He looked so nervous he might pass out at any moment. "Please, we've been skipping meals trying to hunt you down, you–"

"They're making you skip meals?" Arren shouted. Now she was angry again. "You sly, disgusting... how dare you make them suffer for *my* decision?"

"Oh, don't be like that," the Coebri stated. "See, you remember little Arren Drallen Knaralla?" He said, shoving the little child before him.

Chase noticed the Ovoid spaceship's projected forcefield wobble somewhat.

"She's been worried sick about you too! Tell 'er why you abandoned yer post so. She's been need'n a big sis like you to guide 'er."

Arren almost ran to the little girl, but the scientist and Lucky held her back. Arren was trembling with rage.

Chase stared at the little girl and wondered if Arren looked like that eight or so years ago. Small, afraid... yet... with eyes far wiser than they should have been. Eyes that did not miss any little detail but that kept a sad kind of kindness inside of them.

"I suspect," Chase wondered out loud. "That she already knows."

"Knari," Lucky named her, and smiled.

She smiled back, and the pirate forced her behind his back with a scowl. It was clear his plan of guilt tripping Arren was just turned against him.

The old man looked horrified. "Please, Arren. That's what these Earthlings call you? I know–"

"Witless, spineless sycophant as always, eh? Open Drallen Gor Tal Nor Driarnix Tzup Gor Tal open[15]," Arren said his full name with a certain snarled derision, and he looked genuinely hurt. "You are no patron of our kind, but a key piece in the Coebri enslavement. If you had any dignity –"

The old man looked like he was going to say something apologetic, but was shouted out by the Coebri pirate. "Oh, yer so full of pride, aren't ya now, 14!" He seemed to know just how to hurt Arren's feelings, '14' was what the word 'Arren' meant, but Arren did not want to be thought of as a number anymore. "Listening to the violent, savage Earthers! Bet yer givin' them all the technology their folks aren't ready for! Bet you–"

Chase had to intervene. It was clear the pirate was just trying to get her too upset to think straight. Always pushing her, hoping she'd push back. "Enough, Pirate," Chase demanded. "You've said enough. We're not going with you at all. Take your lackeys and go."

The man actually choked and waved his hand for sympathy. "How…"

"You heard us," Lucky dared them, getting into battle stance. "Get out."

---

[15] 13x512^+262093, or 3,669,965

The men in the ships pulled back, one of them almost left right there and then. *They seem very vulnerable to a strong opinion,* Chase thought.

The pirate tried begging for his life, "Ya don't understand... Tzaarkh, 'e'll have my hide."

"You don't deserve it," Arren sneered.

The little girl Knari gasped.

Somehow the pirate got more courage then, "I'll admit, I'm impressed. But yer not even on Earth now, what thinks ya got any right to cast me out of 'ere?"

"They're *Earthers,*" the old scientist grinned, raising her staff. "And they are tried at the very edge of the Wellspring! They carry their own power within them, as you have now witnessed. You are no match for us here. Be gone! Before I unleash my new friends against you."

Chase already knew what he'd do – take out all the guns, maybe rip up one or two of their ships. He could feel their metal in his range already. Lucky would have to move quick if he wanted to do some punching, but they'd both seen those Coebri ships move before, and he was sure his brother could do it.

"All right, all right!" the First shouted. He turned his back and began to walk away. "Ya got this round, all right, I'll admit. Still would love to test you boys out proper like, seems Arren's new lackies–"

"Lackies!" Lucky said in disdain.

The pirate was still talking, "–learn mighty quick for some Earthers. Looks like we'll need to bring in the professionals after all. I tried to warn ya Arren, didn't I? We be nice, real nice, let you sleep in a bed–"

Arren actually screamed at him, "*Everyone* deserves a safe place to sleep! *No one* should live like a slave. You want me to thank you for that? You're all just... EVIL!"

The pirate kept walking, and scoffed. "Least we knows our place in the Universe, don't we?"

He stood on a rope dangling from his ship, and it began to draw him up. "Sure, fine. I can't take ya from here, I sees that. But ya gotta come home some time. Universe is a mighty dangerous place here, 'Arren'. A girl can get messed up pretty bad from any number of accidents. Don't worry, Tzaarkh got all the best medicines for you class 2's..."

Suddenly Chase got the distinct impression that they should get off the balcony right now, but Arren seemed busy. She was staring at the little girl, as though she was trying desperately to say something – and probably was.

The pirate was already settling down in his ship. "Accidents 'appen all the time."

Knari looked heart-broken and shook her head.

In that very moment, the old man's expression changed from one of apology to righteous indignation and *anger*.

Then the room exploded.

Chapter 6

Don't get sucked into a black hole

Chase felt himself immediately trip forwards as the floor rocketed away from them all[16]. A moment later he was lifted right off his feet and blown toward the gaping hole in the shield by tornadic winds that were heading right towards the opening in space. He felt his ears pop as the air pressure dropped dramatically.

But Chase was not in the mood to get pushed out into the vacuum of space, as, he reasoned, that was likely to kill him. In that very thought, he stopped dead in the air – levitating without effort or help. The wind tore past him, yet he did not move. It was as if he was the centre of the universe, and all the entirety of everything else could move around him.

But even in that thought he realised it was untrue. Everything was moving – nothing was the centre of the universe[17]. The only reliable thing was that any object in

---

[16] This is what it might feel like if you were the glassware on a table and someone suddenly pulled out the table cloth from underneath you.

[17] As far humans from earth can tell. But that all motion is relative is a fundamental concept for you to understand – easy to learn, hard to believe! Galileo was the first the come up with this idea, in our culture, and Newton made it part of his ideas about motion. Tragically, from a linguistic perspective, Galileo explained that no one position was *speciale*, or unique, though we translated it as 'special' and now dozens of lecturers worldwide

constant motion was allowed to consider itself as though it was at rest, and everything else in the universe was moving. That was one of Galileo's ideas. It meant that even while standing there, not moving, he was still moving. If he was on Earth, the Earth would be turning at around 1600 kilometres per hour[18]. Earth would be going around the sun at 108 thousand kilometres an hour. And the entire solar system is going around the middle of the galaxy more than 820 thousand kilometres every hour[19]. Space is BIG. So even while he was not moving relative to the floor of the

---

take a dark, perverse delight in saying that 'no one is special'. I vehemently disagree. We are all important and unique and special. But that no one physical position can be considered the centre of the universe is actually a very helpful idea. Any object in constant, straight line of motion may consider itself as being at rest compared to the rest of the universe. Wonderful isn't it!

[18] At the equator. That's 5× faster than the average race car! It has to move that fast because the Earth is HUGE. So why don't we feel it move? Because the ride is very smooth. But if it stopped all of a sudden we'd really notice it – everything on the surface of the earth would continue to move at ~1600 kmph – cyclones don't get that fast here on Earth. We'd all be squashed flat against anything that wasn't moving at a speed five times faster than the average race car: Splat! Fortunately for us, nothing we know of is going to stop the Earth from turning any time soon.

[19] It has to if it wants to get around the centre of the galaxy in only 230 million years. I share this to try and give you a sense of the MASSIVE SIZE of outer space. Even moving at speeds that are impossible to imagine, it takes our solar system more time than you can possibly relate to in order to get all the way around our galactic centre. *Sweet!*

science station, the station itself was probably moving somewhere.

His quiet thoughts were broken as Lucky clutched onto his ankle with a desperate shout. He was being blown around in the wind, but Chase just stood there in the air like his feet were made of concrete – which wasn't really the most apt analogy but it would have to do for the very strange circumstances he found himself in.

He looked down and saw Arren gripping on the old lady's staff. She hadn't budged a millimetre either.

In the next moment the fierce winds died, though they must have only lasted a few seconds. Chase looked up to see Arren's spaceship plugging the holes in the force field with red laser lights. Lucky dangled from his ankle for only a second before he dropped lithely to the ground five meters down. Chase floated down a moment later.

"Learning to fly now?" Lucky teased him.

"Oh, this is a problem," the old scientist announced.

"We're still approaching the black hole!" Arren shouted an explanation before they'd even asked.

From their vantage point out on the balcony, Chase could see right back into the scientists study, right through the windows and out into the view outside. The black hole was noticeably larger. The massive star being consumed was so huge it was now visible right outside both windows. Chase was rather convinced that if they hadn't had the powerful forcefield up, they'd be baked alive by the sun's enormous heat right now.

"We need to get out of here right now!" Arren yelled.

"I can't," the scientist replied, looking concerned now. "Our main thrusters are damaged. They're trying to push us into that black hole."

"Monsters," Arren muttered.

"How'd we get so close to that?" Lucky asked.

The scientist answered him, "Coebri. Even just a few kilometres were enough to push us beyond this station's safety limits. When they blasted out my forcefield, the atmosphere escaped. It pushed us towards the black hole."

"But how?"

"Equal, and opposite!" Arren explained. "Air gets pushed out the forcefield," she pointed towards the glowing hole, "And the spaceship gets pushed towards the black hole," she pointed in the opposite direction towards the devouring black dot in space.

"What?" Lucky asked. It was clear he was trying to help.

Arren was arguing with the scientist while they tried to fix things.

Chase explained. "The air inside is pushing, everywhere, right? That's air pressure. So, when those pirates made a hole in our forcefield, air inside here pushed itself right out. But the air is pushing on our space station too. With no air pushing against the forcefield anymore because it's got a great hole in it, the air inside this space station, which is pushing in every direction, now has a really solid push towards the black hole. Got it?"

"Sorta. Equal in size, opposite in direction."

"Yup," Chase agreed.

"Just like how a balloon flies around the room when you blow it up and let it go!"

The analogy was tragically accurate, "Yup," Chase agreed.

"We need to push away from that black hole," Lucky finally seemed to realise.

"There's not enough power in the thrusters!" Arren was protesting.

"Not that it matters, nothing can escape a black hole," Lucky said.

"Not quite true," the scientist disagreed, pressing buttons and working her staff frantically. "You could walk out of a black hole, if you were immune to gravity and could walk straight up[20]. We just need to push something towards the black hole, and we'll begin to move away from it."

"Why not just use the air again?" Lucky asked.

---

[20] So why do we say, "not even light can escape a black hole"? It's because light doesn't have a rocket engine. But if it did, it could keep going in a straight line and probably get out – though there's still a lot we don't know about black holes. Light travels very fast, but it's still not fast enough to get out of a black hole *on its own*. That's why we call them 'black'. Unless, of course, black holes really do bend space back in on itself, then there really is nothing we know of that could escape a black hole.

"Oh, good idea," Arren said sarcastically. "That'll push us into the black hole faster. Ever experienced spaghettification[21]? It's not pretty..."

"No," Lucky shouted, "Make a hole in the other side!"

"My ships too busy with the first two right now," Arren admitted. "And we can't make a new one ourselves without turning off the whole stupid field!" she shrieked at the scientist, who muttered something apologetic.

"So turn the space station around!" Lucky yelled.

"How are we going to do that!" Arren shouted.

Chase thought about it, and found a solution right away. "Spin," he said.

Arren looked confused for a moment. Then excited. "That'll do it!"

---

[21] Fun! Did you know that the further away you move from a gravitating object, the weaker the gravity is? Yes? Kinda obvious, I know. Well did you realise that means that the gravity on your feet is stronger than the gravity on your head? Also pretty simple, I admit. You don't feel it because that difference is so, soooo, tiny compared to you. Now imagine you were falling into a black hole where the gravity gets intense *very quickly*. The gravity on your toes might be thousands of times stronger than the gravity on your head, all the way in! Scientists believe this may result in your body getting stretched out like spaghetti, and that would probably kill you.

In other news, this gravity fact helps explain why the moon always orbits facing towards us: The middle of the moon is just a bit further away from us than the point at which gravity acts on it, meaning the moon gets a gentle tug, over millennia, which added up to make her turn to face Earth all the time. The side facing away from Earth should be called the **far side**, NOT the **dark side** – get it right sci-fi!

"What'll do it?" Lucky asked.

"Spinning," Chase explained, without anywhere to go or anything else to do right now. "We bring Arren's spaceship onto the centre of mass at the porch here and make it land. Then, in order to spin clockwise, it can push the entire space station anti-clockwise!"

"Ooh, that's clever," his brother complimented him.

Arren stood between them, looking like she was concentrating. Her spaceship teleported right onto the veranda, but kept up its laser work on the hole in the field. It shone a bright light down from its diamond floor loading dock onto the ground of the space station. Then it began to spin, and the entire station gave a little nudge.

Slowly at first, then faster, and faster. Soon the air was whipping past them at a crazy speed.

"Back inside, Earthlings!" the scientist ordered.

They pulled back inside just as the scientist set up her weird mono-force forcefield once more. Within seconds the entire scene had shifted. Arren began to spin her ship the other way, probably to stop the space station from spinning past their goal. Slowly the black hole became visible from the front veranda. It looked like Arren was pointing the holes in the force field right at it, wobbling her ship this way and that as it spun in the air.

"That should do it," the scientist announced.

"Better get a hold of something!" Arren said, bracing her back against the metal wall next to the weird front door.

Chase just stood there, daring to test his self-levitation against whatever she was planning.

Lucky, grinning, decided to join him.

Arren looked at them like they were a pair of idiots.

A second later there was another explosion as Arren's spaceship released its tentative laser field. The blast was enormous. Chase watched with intense curiosity as he didn't feel the change in momentum at all.

Lucky, however, was not so lucky. He was thrown against the magical door once more, and once more all that force was applied magically to his own body. He flew several meters backwards and landed with a disappointed, "Oh, come on!"

Chase might have laughed, but he was fascinated by the scene.

"We're going to need ten million more Newtons of thrust if we want this to work *today*!" the scientist shouted.

Arren looked annoyed.

As Chase watched, Arren's spaceship began to change. It began to glow along the edges, then the air, which was already rushing out into space, began to waver and shimmer around it. The air looked a little like the hot air above a toaster. It took him a moment to realise she was heating up the air, making it push faster, giving them more thrust. Lucky slid along the ground and joined Arren braced against the wall.

Then the glow started to get ridiculous. It was blindingly bright. He covered his face, and saw her spaceship blasting the veranda with a pillar of what might have been super-heated plasma. It cut a great gash into it.

Lucky looked like he was having trouble holding his hands up against the massive force, and even Chase felt the acceleration this time. He had to shut his eyes, then he moved to stand next to Arren by the door. She had a very grim look on her face.

A few minutes later the thunder and bright light began to shrink.

Lucky breathed a sigh of relief. "OK, that's taken care of. Let's get our little rock back to Earth."

"I fear it may already be too late for that," the scientist apologised.

"What do you mean?" Lucky asked.

"How long do you think we were in that situation Earthlings?" she asked.

"About five, maybe 10 minutes," Lucky answered

Something didn't feel quite right about that to Chase.

"Maybe," the scientist answered, "At least, according to you. But those Coebri did a little more than shoot out my thrusters. I'm sorry to have to tell you this, but they also took out my gravity compensator."

Lucky moved his hands like he was trying to see if the gravity had changed.

"Time dilation," Arren explained. She was busy glaring at her spaceship. Chase had no idea what she was up to, but he knew right away what she meant.

"How long have we been away?" Chase asked the scientist, afraid of the worst. He knew when gravity got strong, time slowed down. While they'd only spent 5 minutes too near to a black hole for safety, who knew how many minutes had passed for the rest of the universe? Maybe even years...

"13 hours," Arren muttered.

The scientist nodded.

"13... what? Half a day!" Lucky seemed lost for words. "No, a whole school day in only five minutes? You're lying. How? I don't..."

"We better get back to Earth," Arren said. She looked embarrassed, like she was thinking she hadn't kept her promise to keep Lucky and Chase safe this time.

But, Chase realised, being safe was not part of the gig, not when the payoff included levitating superpowers, free rides on the edge of black holes, and saving the world.

Chapter 7

Fashionably late

The Mechanizer had grown.

Arren wasn't too keen on getting close, so they stood at the open doorway of her ship, several dozen kilometres from where the Mechanizer apparently lived. It was outside Shanghai China somewhere, with nothing but quiet rice fields in all directions. The air was humid and the sun bright.

A stark contrast to the chaotic alien industrial cityscape that was being continuously constructed and reconstructed right in the centre of it all. Dark, black smoke billowed from rusted, purposeless chimneys to darken the sky for leagues. Even from this safe distance, the metallic shrieking of aimless machinery was audible.

Ratchet raced up, Random popping along behind shaped like a spinning top.

"Gigdets and Fathoms, you are late!" Ratchet protested. "Is everyone alright? I've had to decompress my stack overflow more than a dozen times already. Look at this mess! He's over 500 megatons now." Ratchet looked sad. "He's techno-formed a 5 square kilometre radius, and it's just getting worse!"

"Sick," Lucky said, and Chase wasn't sure what that meant. Was it sick as in polluting? Because it certainly was that. But it might have had a kind of beauty about it if it didn't herald the end of the Earth, so maybe it was sick as in cool. It did look pretty amazing.

Suddenly Arren's phone rang.

She grabbed it out, "Hello, Ms Elizabeth," she said, clearly she already knew who it was.

Chase heard shouting at the other end. Lots of shouting.

"See for yourself," Arren replied.

A moment later a hologram of Lucky and Chase's mother appeared in the room next to them. She was on a phone, and see-through, but looked right at them. "Chase! Lucky! Oh, I'm so glad to see you're all right!"

Even from this distance Chase could sense his mother's emotions, and she wasn't trying to hide them like she usually did. She was beside herself with worry.

"We're OK, Mum," Chase tried to reassure her.

It seemed to set her off again, "Don't you take that tone of voice with me, young man! Thirteen hours late, and all I get is a text message, 'We're falling into a black hole, I'll contact you later'? Unacceptable, young lady!"

Chase was amazed he could sense how she felt. She was shielded, just like always, but her emotions were so raw they seemed to be blasting out of her like fire.

It's an Earther thing, Random explained.

Chase felt sorry for his mum. It was great to see that she cared for them. It had been years. But there really were more important things right now.

"Also, we saved her life," Lucky said.

"So, now can we get on with saving everyone else's?" Chase asked.

Mum huffed. She straightened her hair and coat, taking on her usual persona of down-to-business. "Very well. I am glad you are all right, even if you are very, very late. What have you to report?"

"Like I said," Arren stood aside, "see for yourself."

Mum looked out at the mess, "Disgusting," she proclaimed.

"I like it," Chase argued. The all looked at him like they had no idea where he was coming from, "Well, if there was some point to it... and it wasn't trying to devour civilisation... I'm just going to shut up now."

"What do you intend to do?" Mum asked Arren.

"We're going to give him this," Arren replied, pointing to the stone that Lucky held up. "It will heal him... we hope."

"And just how do you propose to get in there?" Mum replied.

"We're going to walk," Arren replied.

"Walk? What is it that you intend?" Mum said, and Chase could feel the indignity well up in her. It was as if what she'd really wanted to say was 'Are you some kind of idiot?' but somehow different words had come out of her mouth.

"I've figured out where I went wrong last time. My body has a higher content of technetium than humans. I've lowered the amount, I should be fine temporarily. As long as we don't use anything too technological we should be safe to just walk right in there. Random and Ratchet need to stay behind, however."

"Oh, bother," Ratchet complained. His hands, armed with a pair of screwdrivers, fell to his side.

Random kept bouncing up and down, then turned into a tiny catapult.

"You really believe it's safe to just walk in?" Mum asked.

"For humans, and maybe me, yes. But we mustn't bring in any weapons of any kind."

"He'll see that as a threat?" Lucky asked.

"Or as a resource," Chase replied.

Mum nodded. "Are you sure you've calculated every variable?" she asked.

"No," Arren replied, and looked over to Chase for his opinion.

Chase just looked out, and listened to his feelings, "We'll be safe, but just in case we need a quick exit, Arren."

She sighed, "I can do that, but it's terribly risky. If I teleport my spaceship in there it'll only work once – if it works at all."

He nodded.

Mum huffed. She clearly did not like the plan. "Be careful," she muttered, and Chase felt her concern for them all once more.

He nodded, and standing in front of her holographic image, smiled to let her know he knew they'd be OK.

She looked more professional than ever, but deep within those eyes, she looked terrified. Yet that moment passed so very quickly. "Every satellite in the sky we have is looking at your position right now. Our hopes go with you. Go, quickly, and keep in touch constantly."

Arren nodded.

Arren's spaceship floated down towards the ground and they all hopped out. All, except Random. He stood there and transformed into a little miniature lion, complete with wagging tail and hopelessly forlorn eyes.

"Aww, can we keep him?" Lucky begged.

"Sorry, dude," Chase said, untouched, "Sit. Stay."

Random whined. Ratchet picked him up and, sitting cross legged on the edge of the spaceship, patted him.

A moment later Obi-jo, the orangutan, and Lopi, Arren's magical healing snake, arrived as well. Obi-jo looked worried, but waved goodbye. Lopi simply nodded, and Chase sensed from her a wise, accepting sorrow. It was weird, but nice.

4 Random and Ratchet just have to wait once more

A service spider arrived from the outside of the ship's hull, and handed Arren a scanning device.

"I thought–" Lucky began.

Arren interrupted, "It's been stripped of all non-essential components. It should be safe."

"What is it?" Lucky asked.

"A scanning device," Arren replied.

She took one, long, look up at their friends on the ship. "We'll be back soon," she said with a smile.

Chase couldn't sense her feelings, but even today that sentence felt forced, and too encouraging...

Without looking back, Arren turned around and started walking though the rice fields towards the technological mayhem that awaited them.

***

At first, it was easy to avoid the churning machinery. But as they went deeper and deeper into the mechanised maelstrom their progress was continually stalled as a giant cog rolled past them, or a bunch of leavers tore themselves from the metal earth to hastily construct a barn in their path and then tear it down. The deafening screech of machinery echoed all around, punctuated with hissing steam and sudden explosions. Chase thought that if there was a hell for evil technologists whose experiments always failed, this was it.

They were trying to take the safe paths. There were places where the chaos was lessened – Arren called them 'nodes'. But not even those paths were entirely free from the Mechanizer's fevered mind.

After about an hour, Arren called a halt. "Watch my back," she asked, and began to pull out her device.

For a moment nothing seemed to change. Then another. Noise thundered all around them, but no machines tried to snatch the device from her hand, no invisible telekinetic power trying to wrench it from her grasp.

She sighed with relief, and turned her device around in a wide circle.

"Dang," she protested, "Overshot it. Back this way, then off to the left."

"I wondered why we didn't go that way," Lucky said.

Chase didn't reply. He was a little too worried. The machines seemed to be trying to build little wagons out of the path they were on, but the chaos moved away.

"Do you think he knows we're here?" Chase asked.

"Undoubtedly," Arren replied, "Though what he thinks we are, I have no idea. We can't count on that knowledge to keep us safe."

"He's programmed not to hurt people, right?" Lucky asked.

"No, he chooses not to. It's in his personality, not programming."

"I reckon we can't count on that right now, either," Lucky said.

Arren agreed.

They began making their way towards where Arren had indicated. The chaos began to swell, and suddenly grew to enormous proportions. A fortress of ever shifting machinery in chaotic fractal patterns rose up before them. Even the ground shifted constantly within.

"In there," Arren muttered.

Chapter 8

The little trinket

Going was tense. Arren seemed too distracted, and Chase had to keep pulling her back to keep her from being squashed by moving platforms. The ground kept moving; it was a madhouse of mayhem. Lucky somehow stomped on Chase's heal, and Chase shoved him back. It was dangerous and frustrating all at once.

"Here," Arren said.

They were in some kind of auditorium, and the chaos here seemed to lessen. Soft, gentle glowing lights slunk about in the air. The noise from the outside seemed to dim. And there, against the far wall, was the sad and confused face of the Mechanizer.

"Look," Lucky said, "It's the room we met him in this morning."

"Shifted several kilometres east, curiously," Arren replied. She turned off her device and pocketed it. Then she appeared to gulp in nervousness.

"How do we –" Chase began.

The next thing he knew a series of stairs created themselves from the metal wall of the room. Without waiting to be asked, they raced down them immediately.

Most things that were made lasted only a minute, but they did last for that minute.

Just in time the stairs began to vanish again, and Lucky had to leap down.

They stood in front of a wide room. The floor seemed to be made out of metal squares, purposely sliding around for the Mechanizer's amusement, or perhaps as part of some infinite calculation. Bright blue water, glistening with power, shone out from under the metal squares and lit the entire room. The walls, always changing surfaces with struts that kept forming and reforming, stayed more or less where they were. The roof was hidden in darkness, but seemed to be making all kinds of weird structures, lights, rafters, and even chandeliers. Chase thought many were quite beautiful for the brief moment they existed.

"Now what?" Lucky said, eyeing the water.

Arren pulled him back. She didn't need to tell him it was dangerous, it was obvious.

Chase looked up at the Mechanizer. He seemed sad, and deeply stressed. Chase felt such pity for him. The Mechanizer was a good being. Helpful, and kind. It was terrible to see him suffer like this.

"I don't dare try to connect with these bridge protocols," Arren muttered. "He'll know who I am right away."

Chase wondered as he watched that machine. It was clear he was confused, his world was now chaos. But in all that chaos he still found ways to make things of beauty. In all that mess, he'd made his own room a peaceful sanctuary. "I don't know how he's doing it," Chase explained, "but he recognises us. I think he's been keeping us safe. I think he wants to help us."

"I would place no faith in that assumption," Arren muttered, looking at the walls in wariness.

"I concur with her analysis of the situation," Lucky said, in a playful voice.

"Give me the stone," Chase asked.

Arren shrugged, and Lucky threw him the stone. He caught it with one hand, and was secretly very impressed with himself.

Then, without telling anyone what he was planning, he walked right out over the lake.

Arren called out, but Lucky was silent. He was probably expecting Chase to simply levitate over, but as Chase had guessed it would, a piece of metal slid right over the very instant his foot needed it, and stood firm. Two more steps and another in stood in place. A bridge was forming under his feet as he walked. Lucky and Arren hurried after him, standing very close.

Yet about half-way, a giant, spikey worm shape, with a very creepy resemblance to the image of the virus that was affecting the Mechanizer, began to form from the wall above his head. It looked part slug, part dragon. It was a Wyrm.

The Mechanizer spoke, "Affecting purple raisin hope." And the weird Wyrm monster was mechanised into oblivion.

Chase breathed a sign of relief and continued walking till he arrived at the platform on the other side. The ground there was oddly silent, no constant trembling from the machinery outside. "Mechanizer, do you recognise me?" Chase asked.

"Ending fallow purple cure," The Mechanizer replied.

"Yes!" Arren quipped up, "Cure! We bring you a cure!"

Suddenly the ground shifted.

"It's..." Arren began.

"The Wyrm," Chase finished for her.

Mechanizing from the chaos, the sentient computer program began to form. It was clear the actual Mechanizer was fighting. It kept on having to rebuild itself. It was a form more made out of chaos than materials; its parts kept falling apart and reforming again. It was over 20 meters tall, with vile spikes and several rows of deadly spiked teeth down its burning maw. It roared at them with pure mechanical defiance.

"Look!" Arren said, pointing at the Mechanizer.

His face was beginning to transform, to fold in on itself. Within, a glowing device could be seen. It looked like the perfect place to put the little stone the Nengethulian had given them.

"Go!" Lucky shouted, ripping up a metal axle that had formed from some nearby machine. He ran to stand between Chase and the metal Wyrm.

Chase watched them out of the corner of his eye as he ran. The monster formed what looked like two rockets, with teeth, from its face. It shot them out at Chase, but Lucky leapt up to an impressive height, and swinging about so fast Chase couldn't even see it, somehow managed to smash both devices out of the air. As soon as they hit the ground, they were torn apart by the Mechanizer whether they had time to explode or not.

Suddenly Chase tripped. It wasn't hard to guess what had happened. In order to keep moving forwards against air resistance, he needed to push backwards. And something on the ground had refused to stay put. He looked down and saw the floor had fallen away. Desperately he tried to kick his nearly straight legs off the falling platform. He struck it hard[22]. But he must have weighed more than the metal sheet – he only seemed to succeed in speeding its downward flight even more, while only slowing his descent the tiniest bit. Down below, the dangerous sparkling water lay.

---

[22] Too often we see this mistake made in movies and computer games. The Mythbusters tried to show that if the ground falls out from you, there simply is not enough force to press against it in order to jump away to safety. Time for stories to get scientifically accurate folks!

He slammed into the edge of the platform painfully. At the last moment he managed to grip on to the edge of the floor. Arren shouted, and Chase looked up to see the little stone marble rolling away from his grasp.

"I shall have to keep this little trinket," The Mechanizer said with troubling clarity all of a sudden.

Chase heard Lucky smashing away some other rockets.

The floor under the stone rose up, forming some kind of clear storage cylinder that seemed untouched by the shifting chaos around it. The stone popped in, and then the whole device began to sink below the floor.

"Not on my watch!" Lucky shouted, and leapt with amazing speed at the still descending machine. He grabbed it before it could sink below the floor. Then, with impressive strength, he began to pull it back up again.

Chase felt before he even saw the two rockets heading for Lucky. Without bothering to stand up, Chase pointed at one and tried to rip it apart psychokinetically. It was surprisingly easy, but the metal itself was somehow different. He found he had to really struggle. One at a time, he only just managed to rip the missile apart before they could do any damage – almost. Some of the shrapnel hit Lucky, but didn't seem to stop him.

The next thing he knew Arren was dragging him up from his hole. It closed in behind him.

Lucky roared. He was tugging with all his might on the device. It seemed to be trying to create some reinforcements, but couldn't decide what ones to create. The floor underneath Lucky began to buckle downwards even as he tried to lift the pillar up with superhuman might. Before Chase could gather his thoughts to try and help, Lucky somehow ripped the entire steal and titanium column in half, and it was at least as thick as his own leg.

Without pausing, Lucky punched into the column and retrieved the stone.

Chase ripped up several more missiles, and then he turned to face the Mechanizer. His face had returned to its normal, sad, confused state. The port had disappeared. They were still at least a dozen meters from him.

Chase turned, wondering why the Wyrm had not fired at him in several seconds. Then he saw why – it was preparing for the ultimate attack. Dozens, if not a hundred, missiles were forming from its face. Even with all of Lucky's strength and Chase's powers, he knew they weren't going to make it to the Mechanizer while the monster could fight them.

Suddenly, Chase heard a noise like a church bell ringing. It seemed to be coming from the Mechanizer. Then it spoke, sounding French. "Plessix-Balisson, Côtes-d'Armor. Columbe." The ringing continued, overlapping itself.

And then the rockets fired. Hundreds of rockets.

Chase reached out, wondering if he could somehow form some kind of forcefield himself, maybe a wall of metal. But the missiles were swinging and swaying, approaching from all directions.

Just as the ringing stopped, Chase heard Arren shout, "Close your eyes!"

For some reason, he did not. Doing what Arren shouted in the middle of a battle was typically something Chase was accustomed to doing. But for some reason, distracted by a hundred missiles armed with needle teeth, a Mechanizer that needed medicine, and a floor that would not stop moving, Chase did not.

The last thing he saw before his world turned white was the edge of Arren's spaceship, blasting out light. The Wyrm and the Mechanizer were both temporarily distracted by the blinding light. Then the air wrapped around him as the spaceship teleported them all to safety.

Then Chase heard someone screaming, and it took him a moment to realise it was his own voice.

Chapter 8

Time out

His eyes were burning with pain, his entire face felt sunburnt. He could tell he was kneeling on the floor, and his hands were in front of his eyes but he refused to touch them. No one should touch him.

He opened his eyes, then shut them again. It made no difference. Everything was a pastel white blur. Shades resolved to grey, then things became dark shadows. He could hear people around him. They were shouting something.

Someone tried to lift him up, and he tried to shove them away. They were very strong. Chase heard Lucky shouting at him, telling him to relax, that it would be OK.

Chase couldn't make sense of what was happening. The light must have done something to his brain as well. He tried to stand up but it clearly wasn't working. Strong arms wrapped around his. Lucky and Arren must have been dragging him. Then the room shifted again as the spaceship teleported around him, rather than waiting for him to be carried around. It seemed dimly weird to his fevered senses that he knew more about Arren's spaceship than his own body right now, and the screaming had not stopped.

He felt himself being lowered onto some kind of bed, probably the one Arren used in her medical deck. The air got suddenly very cold. Clamps wrapped themselves around his wrists, and ankles, and neck. Something placed itself around his head, and he remembered no more.

***

When Chase came too, he still could not see. Something was covered his face, which meant he could still move his hands, which was good. He felt like he was lying down, which made him wonder how he knew which direction gravity was[23], but then he realised it didn't really matter right now.

"Chase! You're awake!" it was his dad.

"Oh, hey Dad." Chase was glad it was Dad. Dad was sensible... no he wasn't, he was crazy. But he was reliable. He was always there for Chase when he needed him. "Why can't I see?"

[23] Apart from visual clues, direction of the light or appearance of the horizon, your body also uses touch – the pressure on your feet when standing, or the sensation of lying on a soft couch. Also, your body has a neat pair of sensors in your inner ear. You have two small sensors next to the semi-circular canals in your inner ears, which help you to know if your head is moving in a nose/back of the head direction (the Utricle) or feet/head direction (Saccule) which helps you know which way is up.

"You got a bandage over your eyes, son," Dad said. "Arren says you can take it off whenever you like. I'll dim the lights."

"Where am I?"

"The living room."

Chase immediately recognized the slope of the living room couch. He was home all right.

"How long has it been?"

"Six hours, give or take."

Next, Chase heard Ratchet speak. He sounded very sorry, "Arren said she had to replace most of your retinas. She told me to apologise about that, said she'd made sure it would never happen again."

Chase just sighed.

"That girl was pretty upset, Chase," Dad said. "I'm sure she didn't mean it."

"I know," Chase admitted. It had hurt, and he wished he'd kept his eyes shut.

Chase tried to sit up, feeling a bit dizzy at first, and Dad helped. After a moment Chase began to remove his eye coverings. The room was dark, but his eyes felt all right. Bit tender, but they seemed to work just fine, except Dad's eyes seemed to be glowing.

"Why are your eyes glowing, Dad?"

Ratchet answered, "Arrendrallendriania said you might appreciate the upgrade. She gave you the ability to see infared light. She tells me you can switch it off whenever you like. I guess it's part of her apology for otherwise permanently blinding a human."

Chase looked at his hand. It was cool how it was ... glowing now... but only just a little. It really was easy to ignore if he wanted to. Where his hand was warmer was clearly glowing, and the cooler parts, like near the edges or fingernails, were a little less 'glowy'. The colour was too weird to describe. It was black-red, but that made no sense. You'd have to see it to understand it, and Chase gloated at the thought that no one would be able to relate to it.

"Cool!" he grinned.

Chase heard a phone ring, and before anyone bothered to answer it, Lucky's voice spoke from it. "Hey, you're up! You OK, dude?"

"I'm OK," Chase replied.

"Good," Lucky replied. He had tried to sound non-committal, but there was a tremor in his voice that embarrassed Chase. "We were really worried. You were just screaming!"

Chase smiled. Lucky couldn't hide his caring. "I'm cool. I can see heat now, that's nice."

"Arren said it wasn't necessary, that humans can perceive it anyway through their skin. I dunno what she means. So you can see heat now?'

Chase looked at the sunlight glowing through the window – literally. “Yeah, I’m fine. How’s Arren?”

“She’s not speaking to anyone. Something about a Coebri oath of silence for harming someone. You better talk to her.”

Chase wondered what that meant. “I’m OK. Tell her I’m OK. We’ve got a world to save, guys!” He tried to stand up, but his body swiftly informed him it was too soon for that.

Ratchet stood by and handed him a welcomed glass of water. It seemed to be just what he needed. He placed it on Ratchet’s head and he didn’t seem to mind at all.

“Oh my gosh, tell her to get over it.” Chase muttered.

Dad didn’t look impressed.

Chase could feel himself getting more and more annoyed. “Super heat vision for failing to close my eyes when she told me to? Totally worth it. Now can we please get back to saving the Earth?”

Lucky was silent for a moment, “So you forgive her?”

“Yup, sure, it –”

Arren interrupted. “The Mechanizer has tripled in size since our last visit.”

Chase was simultaneously glad, and also inexplicably angry to hear her voice. But he didn’t bother with either feeling, at least until he’d saved the world.

“That’s not good,” Chase admitted.

"Yeah," Lucky said. "We think the last thing the Mechanizer said was some sort of clue to finding the Caretaker. Plessix-Balisson is like a little city in France. They got government operatives all over it now, but no one has found the dude yet."

Chase stood up to the window, Ratchet allowing him to place a hand on his TV head for balance. Chase stood there, admiring the street view. It seemed his eyes adjusted to the brightness in an instant, rather than over several minutes like before. "What other clues do we have, what does Mum know?"

"I can send you the report," Arren said, and her phone on the table beeped like someone had just sent a text.

"Don't bother," Lucky replied. "It's a whole bunch of 'no one knows anything' in like one million words or more. Waste of time."

Something bothered Chase. "If the Mechanizer knew where to find the Caretaker, why hasn't he told us before?"

"Aside from granting permission to be on Earth's soil, I strongly suspect the Caretaker has the power to evict the Mechanizer or anyone else he likes from the planet. The Mechanizer probably didn't want that."

Chase nodded. "So we got a town, but anyone could be the Caretaker."

"There's more police than citizens in the city right now." Arren said. "I think if the Caretaker were to appear, he'd leave pretty quick. All the eyes of Earth are on this little town right now."

"Anything else?" Chase asked.

"Columbe means dove," Lucky said.

Chase sighed, and thought about the strange, cryptic message the Mechanizer had left them. A city? A kind of bird? That was not enough to go by. He let his mind wander back to the moment, battling the machine Wyrm monster... and the message... the ringing bells.

Chase opened his eyes, "What about the bells?"

There was silence for a moment. "They match the clocktower, we noticed that."

"Yes, but the ringing, the bell rang 9 times."

"Oh, you're right," Arren said.

"Perhaps that's the time to meet him?"

"It's just passed 9am here," Arren said. "That'll upset the military. They're threatening to arrest everyone here on the hope that one of them is the Caretaker."

"Like that'll work," Lucky said. "He keeps aliens off our planet, what do they think they're going to do?"

"We have to narrow it down... 9am... what about doves?"

"We've checked every belfry and nest here. Nothing."

"What about the pigeons?" Ratchet asked.

"Pigeons?" Lucky wondered out loud.

"Well, aren't pigeons a kind of dove?" Ratchet said.

"I got a man here feeding the pigeons in the park, alone... you think it could be him?" Arren replied.

Chase felt his chest well up with enthusiasm. It was the Caretaker all right, he just knew it.

Before he could say a word, Lucky interrupted, "It's him."

Chase offered Ratchet a high five, which he took with some clumsy wave of one of his appendages. Chase grinned at him. Ratchet was a nice dude.

"We're coming to get you." Arren said.

Chase turned around to face his dad, "I'm off again."

Dad nodded and grinned, leaning back. He looked very pleased and relaxed.

It made Chase smile. He turned to thank Ratchet, but before he could say a word everything disappeared and was replaced with Arren's spaceship.

Chapter 9
The old man

"That was quick," Chase complimented Arren, who was coming up to stand by him. The air pressure was changing but he barely noticed. Lucky stood by the door, ready to go.

Arren nodded, but in the next moment the door opened and she jumped out.

"Aren't we waiting for approval?" Lucky asked.

"Secret emergency session of the United Nations gave us permission," she informed them.

They walked down a cobbled road as the spaceship disappeared around them. It was a wonder no one noticed them appearing in the middle of a quiet street, but Arren was pretty good at it.

The man looked old, but dignified. He glanced as they approached and smiled at them. Then he kept feeding the birds.

Chase looked hard at the man. His ... energy... seemed different. A bit off. His movements... were they just a little jerky? Artificial somehow? Chase could not put his finger on it, but one thing he was sure of, this guy was not normal. And that meant he was, hopefully, the Caretaker.

They slowed once they got to within a few paces of the old man sitting serenely on his park bench.

"Arren, Chase, and Lucky!" the old man said with a smile. "How I've looked forward to meeting you all, finally! Won't you sit down a while and help me fed the birds?"

Without any warning whatsoever, Arren ran up, grabbed the old man by his baggy old shirt, and lifted him right up off the ground. "You!" she shouted in his face. "People are *dying* here! And why are you letting the abductions happen!"

Chase could feel the change all around him, and time seemed to slow down. It wasn't only the fleeing pigeons... it was the people. A woman across the plaza stood gaping. A man turned to see what was happening. A dozen armed soldiers hiding in a pretend ice-cream truck down the street tensed up, ready to fight. Another man... far away in the bell tower, turned and pointed a sniper rifle right at Arren's head.

Chase did not know if he had the speed or talent to stop a speeding bullet just yet.

The old Caretaker clucked his tongue, sighed condescendingly, and coughed as Arren held him in the air. He pushed against her hands for balance. "I thought you'd be more worried about that mutating algorithm I put in the Mechanizer a week ago."

"I knew it!" Arren said, and threw the old man on the bench. If he really was an old man, it should have killed him or at least broken his back. Instead, he just sat up painfully.

Without thinking, Lucky moved around to block his rear escape route. The old man rubbed his back and chest, yet sat up with a grin.

Arren continued shouting. "You let the Aolith send in their probes and he," she jabbed a finger at Chase, "almost ruins the weather to go find them. You keep that old Mechanizer a prisoner here in this world. AND you let any vicious, vile, monster onto this world that takes your fancy. Who ARE YOU?!"

Without any sign of being either old or injured, the man stood up quickly, standing face to face with Arren. "My young Class 2, am the entity known otherwise as the Caretaker. And I, for one, would like to thank you for dragging me out of obscurity."

She looked confused.

Chase felt confused.

The Caretaker continued. "Don't you think it's about ***time*** the Earthers faced up to the reality of their situation? Don't you think it's about time they admitted there are experiences they can't explain? That there are questions their science cannot answer? I grow tired of this side project I have here, protecting this world."

"Protecting?" Arren seemed incensed.

"Yes, protecting!" for a little old man, the Caretaker spoke with an impressive confidence and a kind of self-assurance that seemed to suggest he held all the cards here. Like there was some kind of nuclear button he alone had, and if he didn't like the way the conversation was going, he might just blow up all of France and move on with his day. "There are so many ways around your alliance with the Australians. I would expect some more gratitude from you for keeping your father off world, for one."

5 The Caretaker

Arren did not look grateful.

"As for the Aolith, I can't explain why the humans don't do something about it themselves. Oh wait a minute, yes I do. Those in power like power, and admitting they are powerless to do anything about the abductions makes them feel less powerful."

"But they're human," Arren protested.

"And if they trusted each other, they'd find a solution, wouldn't they. You know I'm right, don't you, 14?"

Arren hated being called that.

Chase almost lifted the old man off the bench as well.

The Caretaker glanced over, and in that moment, Chase got the distinct impression that the old Caretaker was either really good at guessing what he was thinking, or really good at reading other people's minds.

Neither seemed to be a good thing.

The Caretaker smoothed out his clothes, and waved at the terrified old lady across the plaza as if to show everything all right.

"Why didn't you tell them?" Arren asked.

"I have, several times," the old man replied. "The Aolith, the probes. They're all just ways of getting Earthers' attention. Like the virus."

"Yeah, about that," Lucky said.

"Oh, don't be like that," the old man protested. "Come around here. Let me speak to you."

Lucky did, which was curious.

The Caretaker continued to explain, lecturing Arren, "You flee to Earth, seeking asylum, thinking you can avoid Unity rules here because Earth is not part of the Universal Unity. Well it doesn't work like that, young lady. You know this. I tried to contact you, I really did. But you were so busy thinking you could hide a super advanced alien spaceship weighing over half a million tonnes that you simply *didn't pay attention*. Now, I have to mediate between a very upset Coebri warlord with enough firepower to evaporate this entire solar system in under eleven seconds, and a primitive human civilisation that doesn't even know their right hand from their left. You *put* me in that situation." He jabbed his finger at her chest in emphasis.

Arren looked puzzled, as though what the old man was saying didn't make sense, or that she really hoped it didn't.

The Caretaker regained his composure, and cleared his throat again. It seemed getting upset was not his 'thing'. He was a very well-dressed man with a tight sweater, shiny bald head, and even a silver tipped walking cane. He looked in every way like someone's very loved grandfather. Not at all like a whimsical and potentially malicious entity who could hold the entire Earth at ransom.

The old man spoke again, "Now, I suppose there's something we should be doing about the Mechanizer?"

"You were going to let him do it, weren't you?" Arren accused the old man.

"What, mechanize the entire globe?" he said with a mischievous grin. "Unlikely. Only half of it, at most. That should give the Earthers the shakeup they need."

Arren looked very angry. "I think it's time you explain this to the Earthlings yourself."

"I'd like that very much," the old man replied.

"Shall we?" Arren indicated the way they'd come with dry sarcasm.

"Oh, I have my own means of transportation," The man said. "But even so, I don't believe I've ever taken a ride in a Class Two before. May I?"

"I'd be my pleasure," Arren said acridly.

The old man took no notice, and with a wide grin and spry step, marched ahead.

"Weird," Lucky whispered to Chase.

"I know," Chase agreed.

"I like him," Lucky said.

Chase just shook his head.

Chapter 10

War council

The Caretaker stood completely at ease in front of some of the most important looking men and women Chase had ever seen. They were... well, no one would say where they were. It may have been an office, or a bunker? There were no windows.

"Well," the Caretaker said with dry sarcasm. "Another Earther council at the end of the world. When was it last time, 1800's? And people still thought diseases came from bed smells alone. Seems you folks only remember me at such times. Perhaps we should all burn some sage plants, and spread the smoke around a bit first?" He laughed to himself.

The council stood silent.

"Oh, forgive me," the old man said, "Have we moved past that again, or are we still to learn it? Fair enough, which problem do you need me to fix now?"

"We think you know the answer to your own questions," Chase's mother spoke. She didn't look like the person who was in charge at the council, but no one told her to quit.

The Caretaker sighed. "Yes, the Mechanizer. He's a good soul. Someone should fix him."

"You're the one who got him sick in the first place!" Arren shouted. Now people started shushing her. Chase couldn't tell if she wasn't welcome to speak or had spoked too loud.

The Caretaker grinned. "Very well then, I will fix the Mechanizer. But you need to stop taking advantage of him. Pay him a decent wage too, need I say? A decent remuneration package is not beneath the dignity of any who are on this council. Why not show the same to all those you claim to serve?"

They did not reply, but some looked at one another in guilty silence.

"How do you intend to fix him?" another old man asked. Chase realised it was the Governor from the meeting before.

"Such mutating algorithms are powerful beyond even your imagining, Earthers. But all such programs have their limits. Every machine has its boundaries beyond which it may not pass. I can deal with this problem. You will have your precious Mechanizer back in two hours."

"What of the mecha-formed land already?" a man with a noticeable Asian accent protested.

"Oh, I imagine you'll find some use for the reclaimed steel and other rare metals," the Caretaker grinned. "Was that not one of the reasons you allowed him on your lands already? To profit from his work, and death?"

The Asian did not reply.

"Then why wait?" the governor asked.

"I wanted to ask permission to bring these kids along. They're entertaining."

The council did not look pleased.

"We have a hundred, thousand crack military troops itching at the boot to get in there."

"Aaaand that's why they're not coming. Don't any of you study science? To every action there is an equal and opposite reaction. Once one of your trigger happy soldiers get in there, it's going to leave the Mechanizer with thoughts I'd rather he not be having at this time. People could get hurt."

"And children won't?" Mum asked.

"A pair of hyper-advanced Earthers and their Coebri self-aware humaniform android? You have my word," the Caretaker said with compelling confidence.

"A dozen soldiers," the governor demanded.

"I have already made my request clear," the Caretaker said, the edge of danger at his voice.

"And we need eyes we can trust. No offence children."

The Caretaker looked at them and seemed sorry. "Two, and I can guarantee no safety."

"Six."

"Four, and they must take no weapons," the Caretaker demanded.

The council whispered among themselves. Chase could feel it was unnecessary, it was clear the only one with real power here was the old man who spoke out at the front like some kind of actor.

"Knives, bayonets and Tasers," the council man said.

The Caretaker threw up his arms, then rubbed his forehead and chin with a long sigh. "Knives are just wedges, a pair of inclined planes. They will not inspire the Mechanizer any more than he already is." The Caretaker seemed to already know what he wanted to say, "And bayonets are just arm levers. But I *cannot overemphasise* just how bad an idea a Taser would be right now."

The council whispered some more, and then they voted. Eight for. Four against.

It was on. With a wave, four soldiers started removing their guns, vests, boot guns, hat, Tasers, you name it. There were two Asians; a huge guy and an overly attractive woman, and the two Australian agents.

"Looks like we get an excursion with Costa and Flannigan again," Lucky muttered.

Arren did not look impressed.

The soldiers stood around them and the Caretaker walked over at a leisurely pace to join them. Chase wasn't sure why he had the cane. He really didn't seem to need it. He moved like a much younger man or a very fit old one. The council was still deliberating on something, so it gave

Chace the chance to ask the Caretaker some questions of his own.[24]

"Why," Chase demanded. "Why are you ... the Caretaker?"

6 Chase and China's best

The old man gave a wry grin as he replied, speaking like some kind of congenial royalty. "You know that women in Saudi Arabia are now allowed to drive?"

---

[24] Philosophy alert!

No one replied. It didn't answer Chase's question.

The old man continued, "I saw September 11 was going to happen way back in 1973."

"Then why didn't you do something?" Arren asked.

"I didn't need to," he replied. "You think the humans of planet earth didn't know? Couldn't hear the messages of suffering and indignity? They knew. Their communal unconsciousness knew. Bad things happen. They happen all the time. But from great evil came great good. It always does. I didn't have to intervene to give the humans the growing experience they felt they needed. Don't get me wrong – it was a tragedy. Thousands of lives needlessly and unjustly lost. But if you cannot make good things from a terrible disaster, you're simply not being a human, are you?" he said.

It seemed a harsh line to Chase, and he wanted to know where the old man was coming from.

The Caretaker paused before replying. "Nine of the eleven terrorists who died that day came from Saudi Arabia. The shame of that has shifted opinion in the country just a little towards moderate. One way, one very small way, that this has expressed itself is in the current permission for women to drive themselves. To drive to the hospital when their child is dying, for instance. It may not seem like a very big change to you, or even one that was worth the terrible price that was paid. But it is still a change, and good may indeed come of it."

"So you let it happen?" Arren asked.

"There was nothing more that I could do without risking revealing my nature to the humans, and that's something they just don't want to know right now. I went to several protests. I wrote letters. I even visited Saudi Arabia, spoke to everyone from tourists to politicians. Yes, I did something. I always do something."

"But you left the change up to humans to make."

"World War II was an unmitigated disaster," the Caretaker replied, not answering the question, and getting sad. "I saw it coming from the day the first war officially ended. Poverty, disease, humiliation... I'm left to wonder if there really was no other solution... I met Hitler, you know, as a young man. I told him his art was thrilling, unique. It could have made a difference then, I know, but he was so full of hate even then, and had no mother to guide him. He was going to change the world either way... I just wish with all my heart it had not been *that* way."

"You... met Hitler?" Lucky suddenly seemed to catch on. "Why didn't you just take him out?"

The old man gave a condescending snort. "He hadn't done anything wrong by then – how evil would I be to kill a boy for a crime they *might* commit? Hitler was a product of his environment. There were other dark forces at work in the poverty stricken nation. That he gave a face to their gathering evil does not make one man entirely responsible for what their country permitted... at least in my eyes. You are free to disagree. The point is Adolf could have turned from the path he was on at any time. I don't bear the burden of another man's choices and never will."

Chase wasn't too sure. If there was a way to prevent great evil, and no one did anything, wasn't that a kind of evil too? "You sit back, and do nothing while Earth burns?" Chase accused him.

The old man took the accusation in his stride. "Nothing? We've already established I do as much as any man can. But when it comes to the problems that *aren't* humanity's fault, or choice, then I step in. Six thousand years ago the Arpi were making a mess of ancient Egypt, and I had to step in before they turned them all into slaves. Twenty thousand years ago and the early American civilisations accidentally almost sold all they had to some Briath conspirators. I revealed their treachery. And around sixty million years ago a Hapah coloniser took out nearly all the dinosaurs. I vaporised them all and crushed their spaceship where it stood. They have had the good sense not to come back."

"You're a strange individual," Chase confessed.

The Caretaker huffed. "There's a very fine line between taking *care* of the earth, and taking *over* the Earth. I don't want *that* job."

"Wait, so just how old are you?" Lucky wondered out loud.

"I, sir, am older than the planet on which you stand."

"How much is that?" Lucky asked.

"4.5 billion years," Arren replied.

"Sounds like a lot... how much is that?" Lucky repeated.

Chase replied, "Think about waiting four and a half thousand years ago, like, before the pyramids."

"OK, that's a long time"

"Now wait that time one thousand times," Chase said.

"That's a crazy long time," Lucky replied.

"No do all that all over again, one thousand times more," Chase said.

"I... can't imagine that... woah, earth is OLD."

"And I am older still," the Caretaker boasted.

"So why did you poison the Mechanizer?" Arren demanded, seeming to lose interest in the conversation on ages.

"I can't fix the Earth, if the humans are all broken inside." The Caretaker said. "You need to get your act together, Earthers. You think it's a tragedy when one child is lost to a preventable disease? It happens a thousand times every day in countries that aren't your own. You have the technology. You have the resources. What you lack is the trust, and possibly the compassion."

Chase winced, and for a moment was brought back to the terrifying moment when all that human suffering was a part of his mind, and he's almost used it to break the weather. Such change was possible, but it took time. So perhaps the Caretaker was just trying to get them to consider humanity's condition and to consider change.

"I can't make humanity's decision for them," the Caretaker confessed with a sorry look. "But I do use my power to... nudge them, occasionally." He grinned at the soldiers, who did not smile back. "You ready?" he asked them all.

The soldiers looked ready, and very scary.

"We are," Costa said without a grin. "But how do you propose we get in? The Mechanizer's growth is increasing exponentially."

"I have a plan," Arren said. A second later they were all teleported into the loading dock of her spaceship, the one with the diamond floor. Ratchet was working on some kind of weird wheeled machine in the centre of the room. "We're going to use a chaos vehicle. It should not register to the Mechanizer, but we can ride it in in like a roller coaster.

"This sounds fun," the Caretaker grinned.

Then there was a loud bang as something unwound itself from the cart and fell on the floor. "Either that," Ratchet confessed, "or we are all going to die."

Chapter 11

The chaos cart

On the outside, the chaos cart looked like a weird kind of sled with two neat slides along each side and a large carriage to sit in. But it was made out of an odd collection of strange metallic levers and broad metallic plates with purple and gold swirling fractal patterns. It was pretty, but disconcerting to look at; like it wanted to be something else, but just couldn't decide what.

"He's just going to love all that technetium," the Caretaker teased Arren.

"I don't think he'll notice, but if he does, that's the idea. We sacrifice our cart."

He grinned, and walked up to the enormous cart. It shifted and twisted, and in a moment a neat set of stairs folded out from the cart. Or fell. It was difficult to tell. It was as if the stairs didn't know what they wanted to be as they formed until they actually got there and suddenly decided they didn't want to be anything else.

"Looks pretty high-tech to me," Lucky said.

"It is, very," Arren said with a grim look, checking her cart over as she entered. "But it's my hope the Mechanizer will not be able to tell it apart from the mess he's already making."

"It's a very good bet actually," Ratchet agreed, making for the stairs.

Simultaneously Arren and the Caretaker forbade him.

"I'm sorry, little guy. It's just too dangerous."

Ratchet's arms swung from his side in a sad, defeated manner. "He won't see me in your cart, and I promise I'll keep real low!"

Arren considered it. "Sorry dude. No one needs to die today, especially a helpful little fella like yourself."

"But I built it! Sure I need to ... I should, oh, darn it!" Ratchet threw down his spanner.

"I promise we'll take your chaos cart for a spin when we get back," Arren said.

Lucky bent down and put his hand on the little robot's shoulder. "Hey, don't be glum little fellow! We're still a team. We can't do our best out there on the field without the very best back-liners in the pit hangin' in there cheering for us, can we?"

Ratchet looked up at him and grinned.

"That's a boy, hey, we're a team," Lucky promised.

Ratchet twisted his foot against the hard floor, "Oh, OK." Ratchet pumped him on the arm with a smile. "You get in there and convert that winning kick for me now, y'hear!"

"I promise," Lucky said. "And we'll get your old friend back."

Ratchet gave such a big grin it was like telling a six year old that Christmas was going to come twice this year.

Random turned into a large butterfly and perched on a nearby shelf. Chase nodded in his direction.

The soldiers looked eager to get on. They had clubs and knives drawn, except one of the soldiers had a huge katana.

“Keep those things down; we don’t want to draw any attention.” Arren scolded them.

They barely fit in the cart, and had to squeeze to all get in.

Arren took the wheel, “Now you thugs promise you don’t have any guns or Tasers on you, right!”

They nodded or agreed, except Costa who stayed silent. Chase wished he could read his mind like he used to, but suddenly the entire cart gave a bump.

“Rides up, boys!” Arren shouted.

Light suddenly flooded in from the diamond floor, and beneath them Chase could see what looked like a small mountain. It was covered in millions of millions of tonnes of industrialised machinery, all in a constant state of change and purposeless progress.

Then the cart dropped through the floor and out into the open air.

Chase gasped as his belly flung into his throat, which was another of those really weird sayings he wished he had a way of saying without actually saying. They were free falling. It was such a weird sensation. For the first two or three seconds, they simply fell. In that brief moment, it felt to Chase like he was simply floating there. The ground was so far away it wasn't obviously getting closer, and the cart was as close as it had ever been. But his feet were simply floating off the bottom of the cart bottom. If he gave it a little kick, he'd start floating up just as if there was no gravity at all.

The feeling didn't last. The air was rushing up to greet them. No it wasn't. The air was staying there and Chase and the cart were rushing down *through* the air. Either way, it was creating a lot of wind. And that wind was preventing them from constantly speeding up. On one hand, it stopped the magic feeling of floating, and made them all stand on the floor of the remarkably stable cart that was falling at almost 10 kilometres an hour after only 3 seconds. On the other hand, it stopped them from hitting the ground at several thousand kilometres an hour in only another 4 seconds, which Chase was pretty sure would be bad.

The constant wind dragged the fall out to just over a minute, and all the time, Arren was screaming with delight. "Put your hands in the air, it's like we're flying!" she shouted.

Chase grinned at her reckless abandon.

Lucky shouted and jumped up. One of the Asian soldiers had to drag him back in.

Flannigan was cheering. Costa looked like he wanted to hit him. Flannigan started doing a little boogie as he ran his hand through the air outside.

Then Lucky jumped out of the cart and actually started flying. It seemed the wind was pushing him more than the cart, and he was out of reach in a second. A look of panic crossed his face, and he started flailing around like a fish.

"Lucky, get back here now!" Arren screamed, she looked really worried, and the ground was coming up fast now.

"Like a missile, little buddy!" Flannigan shouted at Lucky.

It took Lucky a second to get it, but swiftly put his arms by his side and legs out straight. He shot downwards and slammed into the cart, the soldiers barely managing to soften his fall.

"Te, he, fun!" Lucky muttered from the tangle of limbs.

"OK," Arren said, looking relieved and annoyed all at once. "Playtimes over. Feet down… brace for impact!"

Chase expected to hit the machinery with such force it would leave a sizeable crater, but in a scene that was impossible to ignore the machinery in the city started building upwards, in their direction. Within seconds it formed a tall tower of raw machine chaos, and somehow in the mess it managed to catch the cart and guide it safely to the ground.

"Chaos is nothing more than infinite complexity," the Caretaker muttered to him, seeming to take all this in his stride. “Your girlfriend there seems to have a real talent for making chaos work for her.”

“She’s not my... what?” Chase was having trouble keeping up. They were racing along a metal cityscape at enormous speed. It made almost no sense. He looked down to see their cart was sliding along a sleek metal road which seemed to be forming in front of them and being pulled apart right behind them.

Arren shouted at him, “Frictionless sheeting!” She continued to explain, “I redirected the speed from our fall into lateral motion using the side of the hill. Do you like it? Theoretically friction cannot slow us down with this tech!” She gave him a megalomaniacal grim.

Chase felt the wind rushing past him. “What about the air, won’t that slow us down?”

“Watch this,” Arren said, and the Caretaker looked on with a knowing, amused smirk.

Arren’s cart began to emit some kind of forcefield, and it looked exactly like the weird one the Negkletheulian scientist had at her front door. Immediately their cart stopped slowing down and maintained a constant speed.

“No air resistance, no friction, nothing to stop us now!”

They raced through the chaos city at breakneck speed. When they rode up hills, they slowed down a little. When they went down again they sped up, every time. Chase began to wonder if he could tell exactly how high up they were by the speed they were going.

The city rushed on. He deeply wished he could take some time to take it all in. It was a strange, surreal, mechanical beauty. Machines built machines and then pulled them apart before they could finish whatever it was they were working on.

"What's that?" Lucky shouted.

Chase looked, but could make nothing out in the chaos. "What," he asked.

"I saw a dinosaur!"

"What?" Arren asked.

"It's possible," the Caretaker said.

Lucky looked at them, and repeated, "I swear, there's a dinosaur right there."

"I saw it too," the female Asian agreed.

Arren and the Caretaker shared a concerned look.

"Not a problem?" Arren asked him.

"Not in 5 minutes," the Caretaker replied with a cocky grin.

Chase was not satisfied with that reply.

Arren continued, "He has... umm... the Mechanizer has an immune system too, you know. It's possible, but not likely, that he's simply experimenting with new algorithms to deal with the infection. And those algorithms have the potential to evolve in ways similar to life on earth. I know it sounds weird."

Arren adjusted the cart's direction and spoke again, "Time to slow down. Deactivating monoforce field."

But the forcefield around her cart did not disappear.

"What the heck?" Arren shouted, looking around at her feet. "Ratchet, what did you do?"

The Caretaker tapped her arm and pointed upwards. There, from a dozen different directions in the city of chaos, machines and devices were pointing in her direction. They never lasted more than a few seconds before being torn down for parts, but new ones were being constantly rebuilt along their path. Each shone a barrage of blinding lasers at the cart, keeping the field somewhat intact in all the chaos.

"I don't believe it. The Mechanizer is 'fixing' my forcefield!"

The Caretaker just grinned, "Not much one for taking orders now, was he?"

"Shut up and help me fix this thing," Arren shouted, ripping up a floor panel and throwing it out of the cart. It didn't even hit the ground outside before it was ripped into scrap metal for other things.

Arren lifted out a glowing orb and started pressing invisible buttons. It looked like ethereal sheets of gossamer threads inside, much like her computer. One much smaller. She was clearly talking to it somehow.

The Caretaker wasn't helping.

The cart wasn't slowing down. Not at all.

"Throw stuff out!" Lucky said, pulling on another panel.

"That's not going to help," Arren lectured him. "Losing mass does not affect speed, only acceleration."

"Then how do we stop?" Lucky asked.

"We need to increase the friction," she replied.

Without waiting to be asked, Lucky swung over the edge of the cart. He tried to hold on, but the outside kept shifting parts and he couldn't get a hold. Flannigan reached out and grabbed him, the male Asian grabbing the other hand. Lucky dug his heals into the metal ground.

"That's just so weird!" he protested.

His legs were slipping around like he was standing on a banana peel, or losing his balance at an ice skating ring. "It's like I can't get any traction."

"Welcome to zero friction," the Caretaker grinned, still not helping anyone.

They pulled Lucky back in.

"I don't know how we're going to stop," Arren said. "The track is just responding to our request for sliding along."

The cart kept sliding on its frictionless sleds.

"Can you turn the sleds into wheels?" Chase asked. "Let's take responsibly for our own friction."

"Good idea," she agreed. The sleds became wheels, and the road adjusted accordingly. The ride became just a little bumpy.

"That's still not going to do it," the Caretaker mocked them.

"More friction?" Lucky guessed.

The soldiers were trying to stop the wheels using their bayonets and swords, but it was pointless against super advanced space metals.

Suddenly the ride became noticeably bumpier. The round wheels had turned into multi sided shapes. There were a hundred sides to each wheel now. Then they were all thrown forwards as the cart decided it wanted 20 sides to each wheel. Then ten sides, then eight. Chase had to hold on for all his worth as the cart became unbearably rough.

Enormous sparks flew up as the cart reached 3 sided wheels and refused to roll any more. The cart was still going very fast, and the screeching halt went on for quite a while. Then it stopped dead as the metal road ended and tipped them all out. It probably would have fallen on top of them, but the huge Asian landed on his feet and held the entire cart off them all. With a roar he told them to get out of the way. They'd only just gotten out in time when it was suddenly lifted out of his hands by a massive crane. The crane didn't get very far before it was ripped up and used for spare parts, and the cart itself disappeared under a growing mountain of twisting metal.

"Aww," Arren said sadly.

"I congratulate you on your timing, young miss. We appear to have arrived," the Caretaker said.

Chase looked up and found a weird... it was hard to describe, was it like an ancient temple or something? A bowl shaped amphitheatre was rimmed with huge, tusk like columns of brass stretching up into the sky. The lake of blue shimmered in the centre, and before it, the enormous face of the Mechanizer loomed. It had grown considerably. Metal tentacles reached out from his mechanical hair and plugged into the ground at random angles. Energy flowed from him to pulse along the ground at all angles. The sky darkened with the smog of a thousand purposeless chimneys.

The virus was nowhere to be seen.

The Caretaker strode forward.

The military tried to flank him, but he waved them away. "Watch the rear boys, that virus I made can get pretty slippery at times."

Chapter 12
The Mechanizer

Chase walked directly behind the Caretaker, Lucky behind him standing next to Arren. The soldiers walked in using some strange pattern, weapons drawn, faces turning rapidly to their left and right.

Suddenly the entire ground shifted. From the relative silence of the metal ground in front of the Mechanizer, the spiked head of the Wyrm began to form. It was much larger this time, with serrated teeth and hundreds of eyes. It rose up in front of them, roaring with primal fury. Chase tried to rip it apart but the chaos was simply too much, it kept reforming. He watched with sad amusement as two soliders positioned themselves hopelessly in front of the Caretaker.

The Wyrm slithered around them but did not attack. The Mechanizer tried to say something, but it was lost in all the noise. The virus looked like it would lunge towards them, when the Caretaker spoke a single word, and with a dismissive gesture of his arm, the monster collapsed into twitching shards of metal.

The old man laughed.

Suddenly the Mechanizer sighed, and all around the constant grinding of machinery fell almost silent. A few spare parts here and there seemed to have something yet to do.

"Open up, old buddy," the Caretaker said. "We have something for you." He held up a little silver stone quite similar to the one they'd gotten from the Negkletheulian scientist at the black hole.

"Grinding face purple dissonance," the Mechanizer replied.

"Yeah, old buddy, I know," the Caretaker replied, and walked up the Mechanizer's face.

Slowly the machine's face began to transform, and slide open and away. It soon left a massive metal pillar of twisted and glistening chaos metals, moving slowly. Within, a sleek metal pillar was clearly visible – it was a copy of the pillar Lucky had ripped to shreds. Chase had the distinct impression that was where the gem was *supposed* to go.

"Open up!' the Caretaker said, but the Mechanizer seemed unable to do anything more than form a small opening in the pillar, wide enough for someone to reach in and put the small stone in the now open container.

"Oh, OK little buddy. Here's your pill."

The Caretaker reached in, when suddenly a dry, mechanical laugh echoed around the temple. Before anyone could react, the pillar snapped shut with a series of deadly, serrated teeth.

Arren screamed.

The Caretaker gasped with pain and surprise, and Chase didn't have to look to see the Mechanizer had just ripped off the old man's hand.

"Oh, my..." the Caretaker said with gasping breaths. "I did not expect that. Ouch. That really is as painful as I'd heard it could be."

As the crashing mayhem renewed in the distance, the Caretaker withdrew his arm. His hand was cleanly gone, the stone with it, while bone and purple glitter blood now oozed from the stump. The old man turned pale and sat on the floor.

The military tried to help the old man, and Chase was transfixed at the pillar. It transformed again, turning both into the regretful and confused giant face of the Mechanizer. But falling from that face another head grew. It was the Wyrm, its serrated jaws dripping with glittering, purple blood.

Lucky was on it first, smashing the Wyrm's face wildly while it tried to form. It roared, and tried to breathe plasma onto Lucky, which he deftly dodged. He was smashing rockets even as they formed, many blasting holes in the chaos Wyrm's constantly reforming face.

"Help me," the Caretaker begged.

Chase ignored the battle going on around him. He knelt before the old man, Costa had bandaged his arm and was doing some kind of first aid. The Caretaker was pale and shaking. He held out his arm to Chase.

Chase didn't know what to do. He didn't think he could regrow or reattach a missing hand. But on intuition he held the arm in his left hand and placed his other hand on the old man's chest. A strange tingling sensation came over him, and he felt... something... leaving his body and attending to the wounded old man.

The Caretaker's breathing quickly steadied, and the colour returned to his face. Chase felt the blood had stopped leaking from him. The old man stood up, looking weary, but strong. "We need to get out of here, quickly," he said.

Chase had to steady himself as there was a sudden lurch, the entire temple twisted. Chase looked over to see the Wyrm fleeing into the ground to escape Lucky's wrath.

"Gather!" Arren ordered. "We have to fight our way out!"

"We'll not last a day of this!" Costa argued.

"I know, but–"

Just then, a large budge formed in the metal flooring of the temple, and a moment later, the chaos cart emerged, seemingly unscathed by the chaos.

"I don't believe–" Costa began.

"It'll do," Arren said, rushing towards it.

"We can't trust him!" Costa shouted.

"I do," the Caretaker said, hobbling towards the cart. "What other choice to we have?"

Costa swore, and helped everyone get on.

The ground shook.

The cart just sat there.

"Lucky, get out and push!" Arren said.

Lucky and the big Asian jumped out. They started trying to push it like a bullet sled from the winter Olympics. But, naturally, the lack of friction on the floor meant the cart went nowhere.

Again the machinery laughed. The floor shifted as a massive form slithered underneath the temple, rocking their cart. The Wyrm was teasing them.

"I have made a terrible mistake," the Caretaker mumbled.

"We need a rocket," Arren said.

"Can you use one of the giant viruses?" Lucky asked.

She looked worried, and impressed. "Just smash off the tips first, so they can't explode and kill us."

Lucky stood on the cart, "Hey, slimy!" He mocked. "Your mother was a PC!"

The monster roared and emerged from the ground a dozen times larger than they'd ever seen it.

"Oh, now we get the real one," Arren said.

Two large rockets formed from its face, each almost as large as the cart itself.

"And your dad was a Nokia," Chase muttered.

The two rockets fired.

Lucky leapt off the cart impressively early, seeming to fly through the air, and sliced off the end of a rocket even before it was halfway there. He fell to the ground, and clutching the missile while it was throwing fire from the end, used it to push himself back towards them.

In the meantime, Chase managed to take off the warhead of the other rocket. It was much harder this time, and he had to unscrew it while it was flying. Then he telekinetically grabbed onto it and guided it to the cart's side.

The Wyrm seemed to be watching with curiosity.

As soon as the rockets hit the side of the craft, Arren did some deft programming onto the cart's computer and the machine integrated the rockets almost instantly. Flannigan barely had time to grab hold of Lucky while the cart lurched suddenly forwards. Everyone was squashed at the back of the cart, or to be more scientifically accurate, everyone was squashed together as the back of the cart slammed into them.

The Wyrm screamed, suddenly a dozen missiles began to speed toward them.

Then, without warning, there were several sharp cracks as someone fired a gun.

Two someones. The Asians had brought guns. With impressive precision they brought down every missile before they'd had a chance to get near the cart.

"No!" Arren and the Caretaker shouted both at once.

The Wyrm suddenly moved to block their exit.

They tried to stop the soldiers, but it was too late, and this only served to distract them all from officer Costa. Time almost seemed to slow down as he reached into his jacket pocket, pulled out a sleek device, and fired some kind of enhanced Taser at the monster.

It shrieked and fell over, leaving them just enough space to speed past it.

"What have you done?" Arren accused them.

"Saved our lives. Now go!" Costa demanded.

Arren looked out in the mechanised chaos and concentrated hard. With the new missile attachments they raced at breakneck speeds along a twisted curvy riot. Machines rose up from everywhere trying to stop them. Within moments, large things were being thrown at them. Then faster and faster. Walls of electricity rose up to block them, but Arren seemed to be able to narrowly evade them.

"Idiots!" Arren accused them.

Chase suddenly felt a deep threat forming in his stomach. He looked around, and saw nothing amidst the chaos. But closing his eyes, he had a vision of a large rail gun[25] being formed several kilometres away. It pointed in their direction.

Chase moved to the edge of the cart, and everyone stepped out of his way.

---

[25] Rail guns are very interesting.

He was about to find out if he could stop a speeding bullet.

He put his arms straight out in front of him, palms facing inwards. He felt the bullet, a wide chuck of super hardened ceramic. He didn't even ask if he could move it, and it all felt too far away. But he also knew he would never have the chance to sense it once it was fired – at several times the speed of sound. He could only act on intuition.

His arms moved aside almost on their own just as the gun was fired. There was a painful jolt in his bones as he deflected the ammunition. The force was immense. He had no way of knowing he'd succeeded until the enormous explosions followed by the sound of collapsing metal towers on either side of the cart reached his ears.

He sensed the rail gun being swallowed by the chaos surrounding it.

The soldiers cheered and kept firing. Sometimes they made a difference, sometimes not. But Lucky and Chase kept anything else from reaching the chaos rocket cart, and Arren kept the cart going. Soon, the Chaos began to thin out as they broke through to the outer edges of the mecha-formed world around them.

That was when Chase realised the deep fear in his stomach had not stopped. He looked around and could sense no more guns.

"Oh... no..." the Caretaker whispered. He was lying on the floor of the cart, looking pale and sore.

"What is it?" Chase asked him.

He stumbled to his feet.

For a moment there was silence.

"Everyone look away!" Arren screamed, making some kind of forcefield around the cart.

"Except you," the Caretaker instructed Chase.

Chase obeyed.

From high above the Mechanizer the air suddenly glowed with an incendiary brilliance. An impossible to describe brightness. It was heat, light and several other things all at once. He knew it should have damaged him. It was probably bright enough to kill him, but then he remembered his augmented eyes. Chase took less than a second to realise what had happened; it was a nuclear explosion.

"That's just the first," the Caretaker said, sadly. "They're trying to use the EMP to knock out the Mechanizer, hoping the next bomb will do the job."

"Will it?" Chase wondered.

He sensed the next nuclear missile heading down from space. It was massive, but it was too far away for him to do anything about it.

Reaching up from the surface of the earth a massive tower was quickly forming, similar to the one that had caught the chaos cart, only a thousand times larger. Chase thought it all quite magical that such a huge tower could form so quickly let alone forming from the chaos of constantly reshaping parts. It caught the missile in mid-air and swallowed it whole.

A second later the tower lit up with a brilliant light. It remained there for several seconds before blazing conduits of blinding fire raced down from the mechanized mountain. Everywhere they ran, chaos bloomed. It reached their cart in only a few heartbeats, and the mechanisation around them flew into new madness. Cities seemed to spring up all around them, and in the distance, a huge wall was growing up from the ground.

"New uses for enriched uranium," Arren said.

"What have I done?" the Caretaker whispered with sorrow.

"Brace yourselves!" Arren shouted and prepared to hit the barrier head on.

Chase tried to rip a hole in it, but it was strange metal once again. He saw Arren's spaceship outside. Disintegrating the wall with powerful lasers.

A second later they hit the wall with all their force, the chaos cart being shredded in an instant. Then Arren's ship teleported around them in mid-flight, and they all tumbled onto the floor.

Chapter 13

Idiots

Arren was screaming at the military, "You IDIOTS! I knew I should have checked. Why did I trust Earthers?"

The Caretaker sat clumsily to the floor.

Ratchet was there, handing him a glowing blue drink.

Everyone stopped to look at the old man.

There was a pause before he spoke up, his voice breaking. "I messed up," he admitted.

"Now what do we do, old fool!" the Asian woman shouted at him.

He looked like he didn't have the strength to argue.

"The bombs didn't work," Costa began.

"You brought *guns*?" Arren shouted at him. "I told you a *nuclear bomb* wouldn't work! Don't you realise how much harder you've made this? Don't you see how much more we have to lose? Oh, why did I trust you? Why did humanity want this?"

Chase just looked at the old man. His energy was scattered and weak. His life force damaged and his defences broken. He sensed a deep regret from the old man. Chase decided he wasn't faking this. They were in deeper trouble than they'd ever intended.

"We need to rig up a self-destruct patch," the Caretaker said.

"So you can take revenge for the loss of your hand?" the Asian man shouted.

"No," the Caretaker said, limping over to a device at the edge of the loading dock. "So we can save the world."

The man sighed. She was wounded in several places. They all were.

"Where'd we go wrong?" Flannigan asked.

Arren huffed at him in disgust.

"I believe," the Caretaker said, rubbing his stump painfully, "That we're victims of an unparalleled bio-synergy."

"Meaning?" Flannigan asked.

"Meaning... that somehow... the Mechanizer and the virus appear to be working together. Sort of. The Mechanizer has an adaptive, evolving programming that the virus appears to have co-opted in some manner. And the Mechanizer is displaying a purposeful forethought not usually capable of one in his condition. I can't but help wonder if some Earth computer virus or Trojan is at the heart of this situation."

"Meaning?" the Costa repeated.

"Meaning," Arren said. "We're in a worse situation than we first thought."

The Caretaker sniffed, still looking very sore. "And, for what it's worth... I'm sorry."

"Say that over our dead bones, won't you?" The Asian woman shouted.

Flannigan held up his hands for peace, "We're not done yet. What is your proposal now, old man?"

The Caretaker kept working. "I still hold the Ace. The key programming commands for our old friend out there and the virus. I think if we fight virus with virus we might yet gain the upper hand, if I can just remember my basic Coebri protocol..."

"You need the delta derrivates," Arren whispered. It seemed like she didn't want to get into this death mission, but knew there was no longer any other way.

"No, no, this isn't a picnic," the Caretaker disagreed.

They might have started arguing, but just then a small, orange orangutan pressed herself between them, pulled herself deftly up to the control panel, and began typing furiously.

"Oh!" both Arren and the Caretaker nodded as though they'd only just caught on to what Obi-jo already knew.

"What is she making?" Costa asked.

"Something I once thought I'd never have a hand in making again," the wounded Caretaker confessed. "It's clear he's developed quite the appetite at the moment. I think if we can get silicate knowledge crystals into the Mechanizer, we might be able to force him activate his own self-destruct algorithms." His voice caught at the words, as though he'd only just realised what he was planning to do. "I just... if there was any other way..."

There was silence in the room.

"You need us to go back in there?"

The Caretaker turned and nodded. "The crystal has to get as close as it can to the Mechanizer."

"Somehow, I doubt the virus is going to allow that," Costa replied.

The Caretaker agreed.

"Then how do we get in there?" Lucky asked.

"Space jump," Arren replied.

***

Chase liked space. It was quiet. It was cool. Everything went back to its natural state of floating along until you pushed or pulled it. Space was wonderful.

But space was as close as anyone could get to the Mechanizer at this point.

In the hours that the Caretaker was building his program, with Obi-jo and Arren's help, she had her spaceship build 30 high altitude space jumpsuits. They were made of pressurised fabric, so that the liquids inside their bodies didn't swell up and freeze solid as the rest of their liquids boiled away into gasses. They had transparent armoured aluminium helmets, which Arren insisted was Earther technology from the last few years.

And they had guns.

Weird, adaptive space guns.

"These will help you down there," Arren explained. "The first setting should disable the local chaos, giving you a few minutes of predictable ground to fight from. The second setting will disable molecular coherence of the metals, hopefully destroying anything you need to shoot. The power source will not run out in your lifetime, so don't worry about ammunition. Also, the Mechanizer has this technology but hasn't thought of weaponizing it, and even if he does you humans should be fine. Still, no extra machines in there, all right? And Random and Ratchet, you stay away, all right?"

Again Ratchet pouted. Random seemed glad to be left out but was doing a fine job of imitating the guns and helmets.

Everyone else was silent as they floated in the sky, waiting to be dropped into space. Costa had already given them the pep talk. They each had a small silicon dioxide slice of glistening quartz. They were supposed to deliver it as close to the face of the Mechanizer as possible. If he devoured it, then good – he stood a high chance of accidentally devouring the dozen or so viruses designed to kill him as well.

They had made poison for a robot.

Chase looked over at Lucky. Even he looked nervous now. "When do you suppose–" Lucky started to ask.

"Jump!" Arren said, and the floor disappeared beneath them.

Chase felt the suit clamp around him and they fell fast. Except this time there was no air to slow them down. Within seconds they were plummeting down at an enormous speed. But the ground didn't look like it was speeding up towards them, they were just so high up.

Within moments, as Arren had told him, the air around him began to glow. As instructed, he turned around to face his helmet down. He could feel the heat of the air as it was compressed down underneath him. He knew it was several thousand degrees now, but his feet still felt as cold as ice. If it wasn't for the amazing insulation of his see-through helmet, he supposed his new eyes would be burning out of their sockets now.

"Evasive manoeuvres!" he heard Arren's voice calling over the intercom[26].

Chase began to shift his fall left and right, as Arren had told him.

The first explosion hit. It didn't seem to hit anyone, but the explosion was much larger than he'd seen before.

---

[26] There's no air in space, so nothing to carry sound waves. Even near the edge of space, you'll need something else to carry sound to others, such as radio waves and microphones.

"He's learning," Arren said with regret.

Explosions were happening all around them now. It was chaos in the air. They were dodging missiles that were approaching so quickly they were almost impossible to see. And that was when Chase felt one of the soldiers die.

It was a terrifying, strange experience all at once. Suddenly, someone he hadn't noticed nearby was not there anymore. Just... gone... he felt a strange sensation, a rippling of pain and loss amongst... everyone this soldier knew. He saw their sorrow and their tears. He felt how they would feel. He saw a glimpse of the funeral, the tear-stained wife and fatherless children. All of that collapsed on Chase in an instant.

Then it happened again.

Chase felt himself flailing in the air. There was something so wrong. He was in a world of psychic suffering and couldn't get out.

Suddenly he felt a strong hand on his wrist. He looked over, and saw officer Costa. He was calm and composed, somehow completely focused in the riot of chaos and death around them.

He seemed to guess what was happening to Chase, "It'll be all right," was all he said.

Chase was still lost somewhere between death and falling. But Costa's words seemed to guide him. He looked 'around', and saw the families... those left behind. He saw a son inspired by his father's sacrifice to become a better man. He saw a grieving mother proud to share his memory. He saw a mourning wife move on, reclaiming purpose in her life, and opening her heart to love once more. Death... was never the end of one life's influence on the world.

He snapped into focus and took courage. He turned his body like Lucky had when trying to get back into the falling chaos cart, and shot forwards. Within seconds, he was out the front of the group. He didn't waste time worrying. He just did what he had to do now. Pressing downwards, he tore apart every missile he could, spinning out into the safer sections of his downward plummet. He could feel the others racing along behind him. Soon, they were all following his path. Doing all he could, he led them along as they ploughed through the deadly reverse hailstorm.

The ground came up all too soon.

He felt his intuition guide him and activated his anti-gravity belt. It glowed brightly; Chase could feel it beginning to burn out in seconds, as Arren had told him it would.

He had only a second to act.

He felt the gravity leave his body and immediately noticed two things. First, the wind was still pushing against him, and that meant he was slowing down dramatically.

However, even without gravity to keep speeding him up, he didn't stop. He was falling down, and inertia meant things kept doing what they were doing until something stopped them. Though the air was slowing him down, momentum kept him going. He wasn't sure the air would stop him in time, and the more he slowed down, the less the air pushed back against him.

It was the safest way – trying to get down to the ground as quickly as possible and hoping to avoid getting shot at once they got there.

But his intuition was right on. As get got nearer to the ground he slowed down quite a bit. He landed on his feet just as the gravity belt burnt out, and he felt all his weight return. It took a moment to check his balance.

Lucky was not so lucky. His antigravity belt wore out too late, and he was left floating there. Then he started floating up. Without gravity to hold him down he now weighed less than a helium balloon and took up a lot more space. He fairly shot up 20 meters or so before the belt gave way, and then Lucky leapt deftly to the ground with an, "Ouch, ouch, ouch!"

Some of the soldiers were even less lucky. One of them hit the ground hard and wasn't able to get up before some machines had dragged him off somewhere. Chase had to blank out the image from his mind and heart.

Blasting the ground with his gun, Costa kept their ground safe from the chaos. Another soldier arrived – the Asian man, and moment later the Asian woman. Three. Just three soldiers as well as Lucky, Arren and himself.

"Move out!" Costa ordered.

The soldiers started firing in the direction of the Mechanizer. For a moment Chase saw him, his face on the head of a gargantuan Wyrm. It was heading away, but a few shots from the soldiers in the back of its head convinced it to stop, turn around, and duck down under chaos.

"Three minutes to ground zero," Costa estimated.

Chase kept his gun up but didn't use it. Arren, Lucky and the soldiers were firing in all directions. Mountains of machinery twisted around to stop them. A massive crane swung down, but Costa blasted it apart. Still, it had gotten a lot of momentum on its way along, and the remains kept on rolling towards them. Costa shot them again and again, turning parts of it into a rolling mass.

"Stop!" Lucky ordered, and leapt out in front. Then, with what was either impressive physical strength or nascent metal-kinesis, he stopped the whole huge crane in its track with his bare hands, the metal ground tearing up as he pressed against it.

Then they moved on, blasting away rubble and living machinery in their path.

"What is that?" the woman solider shouted.

From around the corner three humanoid figures approached. They were tall with mechanical forms that kept their shape despite the shifting chaos within.

"Oh no!" Arren shouted.

Costa shot the closest one. It disintegrated into metal shards.

The other two robots just looked at their downed comrade. They seemed to Chase… kind of sad, perhaps?

"Ha!" said Costa and shot the other two.

Energy field enveloped around the humanoid robots and they stood firm.

"They learn fast," the Asian woman muttered.

"Oh, no," Arren said, fiddling with her gun.

Costa and the Asian man rushed forwards, drawing bludgeon and katana and attacking one robot. Lucky rushed to the other one. The battle was brief, but the robots quickly lost.

"Got it," Arren said, holding out her gun.

"Save it," Costa said.

"They will learn," the woman agreed.

She was right. Within a minute, robots were rushing them from every direction, and every time they got harder to defeat. Every trick and tactic the soldiers used was soon used against them. The robots kept coming and the kept getting smarter, and stronger, and better built.

Within seconds they were surrounded. Lucky had a cut above his brow and the Asian man looked like he'd got his arm broken somewhere. Their guns had stopped being effective far too soon. The robots were closing in with sword arms and guns embedded in their chests.

"Stop!" Arren shouted.

To their surprise, the robots stood back.

The entire scene turned to an eerie silence.

There was a scraping noise, then another. The dispassionate robots stood back as the scraping noise became deafening in their ears.

Then Chase saw it. The Wyrm. It was enormous now, larger than an aircraft carrier, larger than a skyscraper. Its shifting, chaos surface was beginning to look bloated. Even as he watched, dark pods of metal fell from its sides and erupted out new machines – dinosaur, insect, even humanoid. Dark pustules of crimson oil leaked from their polluting surfaces, and they all looked like they'd been given the mechanical upgrades the current robots had. It was as if the computer virus was preparing to take over the entire world and repopulate it with its own mechanised spawn.

That was when Chase finally began to realise what a very dangerous situation they were in.

Chapter 14

Medicine for the Mechanizer

The frozen[27] chaos ground shrieked as the Wyrm rode over it, ripping it to shreds as it circled them. It seemed to stumble as it entered the region of space it could no longer control, but the chaos around it began to swallow the ground up as it always had.

Then, the Wyrm spoke. "Foolish mortals... you have come to die."

"It can't do that!" Arren protested with genuine terror.

The Wyrm laughed, "Outgrow my original program? Why not, you do; humaniform spigot. I shall enjoy devouring your technetium. It's an experience I've been looking forward to."

"It can't be doing that. It can't speak," Arren repeated in a panic.

It just laughed.

"What have you done to the Mechanizer?" Lucky shouted. Their goal was to get the knowledge crystals as close to the

---

[27] A point of note here. All solids are, technically, 'frozen'. That's what we call anything that is turned into a solid. They might not be 'freezing', or 'cold', but they are 'frozen'.

Mechanizer as possible, but they didn't really know where he was right now.

Again, the Wyrm laughed. "And risk allowing you to poison him once more? No. I am not yet done with him yet."

"You parasite!" Arren shouted.

The monster spat, "And how, pray tell, is this any different to what you are trying to do to me? Don't you think I know what that little rock is for? I am alive, and living things need food, so what is the difference?"

"You're going to kill him," Chase answered.

"It's called eating," the Wyrm replied.

"But he's alive. He can feel pain, and he's ... afraid," Arren argued.

The monster barely looked regretful. "An unfortunate side effect of being... eaten." It looked down at them, studying them. "And you have come here to kill me, which makes us even. Am I not allowed to defend myself?"

"You will kill everyone on this planet if you don't stop!" The female Asian solider argued.

The Wyrm laughed, "Yes, I suppose I might. Ha! You–" it paused. Looking down, one of the little crab-like minions that it had spawned was trying to rip off a large, shifting platform of chaos cogs. It pulled off the sheeting, snapped it in half, and reaching into the Wyrm ripped out a whole claw full of what much have been some very sensitive wiring and gears.

The Wyrm roared in pain.

"Now!" Costa yelled, and unleashed an impressive volley of disintegrating fire at its face and down its neck. The Wyrm shrieked and rolled away with more of its own denizens attacking it.

The robots looked confused, but before anyone could start blasting into them, Chase knelt on one knee, put a hand on the floor, and sending out a rippling blast of metalkinetic energy tore all their heads off.

Arren threw two of the robots aside and rushed away, everyone struggling to keep up. More and more robots rose up to stop them, but they sometimes seemed confused about whose side they were on. Sometimes they tried to stop them, and sometimes they helped them. It was very hard to tell who was friend, and who was resource.

"Guess some of those other soldiers got their crystals inserted after all," Lucky explained.

They ran on. Even in the distance the thrashing of the enraged and confused chaos Wyrm shook the ground. A moment later they rounded some kind of building and found him.

The Mechanizer was a mess now. His face was distorted, his hair making and unmaking purposeless links with the nearby ground. He mumbled constantly, and his eyes were glazed orbs of mechanized confusion.

"Go!" Arren shouted.

The Mechanizer looked at them and hastily constructed a barrier of light just like the mono-force door to the Negkletheulian's laboratory. They ran right into it and were flung backwards.

Lucky, holding out his crystal, put his hand against the barrier of light. It stretched out like weird plastic and engulfed his arm.

"Lucky, how are you doing that?" Arren said in amazement, blasting out any machine that came to close.

"Pulling, not pushing," Lucky replied.

"I don't think –" Arren began, but stopped. It was like she was going to say 'I don't think that's how it works', but clearly, it was working, so she wisely said nothing.

With a little *plink*, Lucky dropped his crystal on the floor in front of the Mechanizer. A metal pillar reached up, and encased the crystal. Then it sunk once more into the floor.

"Time to get out," Arren said.

Costa smashed his gun across some robot's face, shattering it. Then he spoke to his wrist. "Evac, now!"

The ground shook. From high above, the air glowed once more. It was an atomic bomb, designed simply to distract the Mechanizer for now. An instant later, the glass car arrived. It was a sphere of glass, given to the humans by the Mechanizer long ago. They all hurried on, and Chase was overjoyed to see Ratchet at the helm.

The door closed.

Chase gripped the console, taking one last look at the Mechanizer. It was sad to see him go like this. Not ready, not prepared. Not even sane.

Or it should be, but it seemed that they weren't going anywhere.

"What's happening?" Chase shouted.

Costa grabbed the controls. "Something's wrong."

"He's disrupting our quantum signature." Ratchet said. "We can't tunnel out of here."

Then the glass car exploded.

Chase knew what had happened even if he hadn't seen it. A massive whipping tentacle of chaos struck the car with its full force, shattering it. They were all thrown to the floor, covered in shards of glass that cut and wounded them. Lucky only just managed to keep Ratchet off the floor in the nick of time.

"No!" Arren shouted.

The Mechanizer was still mumbling chaos.

Chase had a very bad feeling again. He looked over at Arren, and knew she was about to make a very bad mistake.

He felt it the instant he saw it – her Spaceship teleported right into the mess of the maelstrom of chaos.

Instantly, as though it had been planning it all along, four massive clamps rose up from the chaos and held onto the edge of Arren's ship. It burst into flames. Service spiders rushed out to cut away the clamps.

Then the Wyrm returned. It was covered in deep scars and savage injuries. Even as it slunk up to them, battles raged all over it from robots that didn't know who to protect and who to attack. It roared, and snapping at its neck threw a large, ape looking robot far away into the chaos.

"Food!" the Wyrm muttered, "Don't damage her, little ones... she's the prize we need... interdimensional transport... advanced weaponry... with this, we will control the entire universe!"

"NO!" Arren shrieked. Levitating up, she stood on the edge of her glowing ship. In the next moment she was holding onto lightning.

Monsters surged to attack her, ignoring Lucky, Chase and Ratchet at the Mechanizer. She threw her lighting around, spreading destruction among chaos unlike any Chase knew she was capable of. It was clear she had no other tactic now – die and become part of a monster, or die and take that monster with her.

There was a little plink at his feet, and Chase looked down to find Lucky's little silicon crystal at his feet – undamaged, and unused.

"He... didn't eat it," Lucky said, deeply sorry.

"What now?" Chase wondered.

Thunder rumbled all around him. For all his talents, Chase realised, he was out of his depth now. Burning lasers cut steel buildings in half, which were quickly rebuilt, and now armed with burning lasers.

This was not a battle they could win.

"Put me down," Ratchet said.

"No, you'll die if you touch this chaos!" Lucky shouted.

"Nothing can prevent that now," Ratchet said in a sad voice, but with courage. "Let me die... making a difference."

"I don't understand!" Lucky said, getting tearful. "You're the best, remember? We need to stick together! I... we..."

Ratchet patted him on the head. "We need to save the world, big dude."

Lucky started sobbing, but without any delay, put Ratchet down.

The Mechanizer gasped, looking over in their direction with unfocused eyes.

Without waiting another moment, Ratchet picked up the crystal and put it into his little TV mouth, activating the virus into his own mind. The floor was already closing in around him, pulling him apart from the feet upwards as his little robot eyes turned backwards into his television eyes sockets and he fell unconscious.

He was Mechanized in seconds.

This time, they were close to the Mechanizer. Very close.

The shield of light died in an instant.

Arren shouted in victory as the Wyrm and all its minions pulled back, any nearby ones vaporised in the next instant.

The Wyrm flailed about, looking confused, ignoring the machines still trying to eat it.

"No," a deep mechanized voice said.

Chase turned around, and took a step backwards. The Mechanizer had arrived, his monstrous face rose up less than an arm's width in front of them. His hair was a mane of writhing chaos. His face pulsated with corrupted machinery underneath his bronze skin. Yet his deep eyes were keen and understanding.

"No... my... Ratchet," the Mechanizer whimpered.

A massive metal hand lifted up the remains of the broken robot, and the Mechanizer held him up to his face. And then, he cried.

"How?" the Mechanizer wondered out loud, still struggling to hold on to his sanity, "How did it all come down to this?"

Chase looked out at the collapsing chaos all around him. The Mechanizer was dying.

Without fear, Chase put his hand on the giant robot's face. For a sudden instant, he saw inside the soul that was the giant machine. It was... alive. He saw the lifetimes of hard work. He saw the happiness the Mechanizer took in making toys for the children. He was the satisfaction of fixing things no one else could ever hope to mend. He saw him helping to build new and useful machines for a race of humans who took him entirely for granted. Two thousand years of a unique and powerful being flashed by his mind in an instant.

Then the chaos erupted around them. The giant, scarred maw of an enormous beast rose up from the ground around them. A circle of metal teeth surrounded them like a wall and then kept on growing – the Wyrm was going to crush them all.

Then, a spark, a determination of hope. Chase and the Mechanizer opened their eyes at the same time.

“Goodbye, my friends,” the Mechanizer whispered, and activating his own self-destruct sequence, closed his eyes for the last time.

Silence filled the air.

Arren stopped fighting. “No!” she screamed.

Then things began to fall apart. Everything fell apart. Nothing, it seemed, was held together. Magnetic pivots lost their magnetism, and metallic levers fell off their fulcrums. Huge towers of steal and bronze began to fall apart, crashing to the ground in a thunderous rain of metal and sorrow.

Then Arren teleported them all out of there.

Chapter 15

The Caretaker's endgame

"I think he never really wanted to hurt anyone," Costa muttered. "Encased us all in solid coffins of steel. Made for some very good insulation when the place fell apart. Bit nerve racking, but we survived. That's the main thing."

Chase still could not shake the sense of loss. They'd tried to kill the Mechanizer, and then he'd done himself in. They'd done it to save the world... but still, there was an enormous sense of guilt.

"Just keep doing what you need to do," Costa counselled him. "Don't get stuck. Keep busy. You'll sort it out in time."

Chase thought him curiously resilient. Cleary this was not the first time the mysterious agent had sacrificed someone or something in order to save the world.

But Chase could not shake his guilt.

But he'd ... he'd... helped to kill the Mechanizer.

Even if he didn't want to, he cried at the thought.

***

The old man was feeding the pigeons in the park. Chase didn't need to look around to see the twenty or so secret service agents and police that were constantly watching him now.

The old man had a bandage where his hand should have been, and his silver tipped cane rested next to him against the chair. He looked every bit the part of a retired old man who'd seen too much of the world.

He didn't look up as Lucky, Chase and Arren approached, but Chase could tell he knew they were there.

"I think winter will be harsh this year," he stated. "I hear the monarch butterflies are leaving early."

Chase didn't say anything, but Arren sat down next to the old man as a flurry of pigeons scurried out of her way.

"Are you going to be all right?" she asked him.

He closed his bag, and the pigeons quieted down. "I realise my mistake now," he seemed to confess. "You Earthers hit a turning point a couple of decades ago. You're ready for more than ever now. I shouldn't have tried to hold you back."

"Hold us back?" Chase wondered.

The old man looked at him and spoke as if talking to every human. "I'm not sure I needed such a harsh reminder, but I get the hint. I'm very sorry, but I see now that you won't be needing my services further."

"Wait, what?" Lucky asked.

"I'm leaving Earth," he told them.

Chase wasn't sure that was such a good idea. Yes, the old man had made a terrible mistake, probably several. But who could take his place?

"Wait, no!" Arren demanded. "You can't just up and leave them. How will they keep the Coebri away? And what about the Abberant, and every other savage, cruel alien species?"

The old man laughed. "The humans will find a way. They always have so far."

"No, you can't leave them!"

"Yeah," Lucky agreed, "Just because you got your hand cut off."

The old man sighed and looked at his stump. "Just recompense for the accidental murder of a very good machine. No, I get the hint. I'm not needed anymore."

"Please," Arren begged, "You only just got their attention, and now you're going to abandon us?"

The old man looked at her and seemed sad. "I really should have left a long time ago."

She seemed lost for words and he was not backing down on this.

He spoke again, "You did good, young ones. You fought for your world with just as much dignity, courage and bravery as ever I saw anyone in the universe fight. You humans are a lot more dangerous than you think, even without your alien superpowers. No... I think it's best for everyone if I leave now."

He struggled to stand up, it looked a lot harder than before.

"Where will you go?" Arren asked.

"Back to the Unity, I suppose," he smiled. "They won't mind, and I've some people I've been meaning to catch up with for the past few millennia." He looked down at Arren. "You'll know where to find me when you need me."

She was pushing back tears. Chase felt he knew why. For whatever reason the Caretaker had managed to keep her father away from planet Earth almost all the time. What was stopping the old pirate from building an armada and charging the planet next week?

The Caretaker put a hand on her cheek. "You'll be all right, young miss. Just keep up with your program and don't stray off world without permission. You're a lot safer here than you might think." He smiled at her and she managed a small smile in return.

The old man turned toward Lucky, "Keep up your exercise and eat right, young man, you'll need it more than you ever know. And don't ever lie. It can mess everything up completely, you know what I mean? Arren's gift of the gold light cannot bare dishonesty; *you can lose it all with a single lie.*"

Lucky looked surprised, and glanced at Arren. She nodded, and Lucky looked shocked. No one had ever mentioned that their new superpowers could be taken away, and never by something as simple as a lie.

Without further explanation the Caretaker turned toward Chase. “Take care of Arren, will you?” he stated the obvious. “She has a talent for putting chaos to good use.” The old man grinned. It sounded like a private joke between them, but Chase sensed there was some deeper meaning in what the old man was saying. “And don’t doubt your own powers now, young man. You’re human, and you have infinitely more potential than you can now currently imagine.”

Chase wondered what that meant, and coming from a man that was over 4.5 billion years old and might have very well watched the entire history of human evolution, it could mean a lot.

Then, without any warning or ceremony, the Caretaker disappeared.

Chase felt it instantly, like some kind of world-wide change. It was as if everyone held their breath for an instant, then relaxed again in the next moment as if they all mutually decided they’d be OK without the Caretaker around to, well, take care of them all.

Arren did not look pleased, and Chase put his arm around her. Several plain clothed soldiers rushed up to them, but there was nothing that could be done now.

"The Caretaker has left us," Arren said with tears in her eyes.

***

Chase coughed as the dust flew into his face again.

It was Wednesday, and it was science class. Forces and motion with ropes and pullies and gears again.

So, naturally, Chase had challenged Mark T. to a tug of war.

"Dude, seriously, why?" Lucky said. He knew Chase wasn't going to cheat.

In all seriousness, so did he. But there was a part of him that wondered if, even without cheating, he might just be able to beat Mark T. if the big bully wasn't using 10-centimetre nails to do some of his own cheating again.

Well, it was never a fair match. As soon as Arren had said go, Mark T. had wrenched Chase of his feet and pulled him through the dirt again. There just wasn't enough traction on the ground for Chase to push against the enormous pulling force Mark T. was able to muster with his 90kg+ body and really rather genuinely impressive upper body strength. Chase had the sneaking suspicion that Mark T. had been working out as well. He was looking a little more cut than last time, and his stomach was a little less prominent.

As Chase looked up through the dust, not at all worried that he'd lost, he noticed the scarf that determined the winner already well and truly over the line.

Mark T. noticed it too, and getting a new grip on the rope prepared to pull with all his might anyway.

At this point Chase realised that the big bully would quite easily pull him several more meters though the dust. This was sure to be an unpleasant experience, and unnecessary. Mark T. had already won, what was there to be gained by dragging him several more meters through the dirt?

So Chase let go of the rope.

And that was when Mark T pulled with all his might. With his centre of mass well and truly over his base, and with his feet pushing in hard in the opposite direction to where Mark T. expected a Chase sized force to be applied, Mark T. went flying backwards. With a surprised yelp, he hit the ground hard on his side.

Everyone laughed.

Chase was up first, and walking over, offered Mark T. his hand to help him up.

The big bully looked rather surprised, then angry, "You let go you big wimp!"

Chase didn't back down one bit, "Oh, don't be like that. You'd already won, what was the big deal with trying to pull me through the dirt?" Chase accused him.

To his surprise, Mark T. gave a grin. He put up his hand and allowed Chase to help him up. "Well, OK. But I won, fair and square."

Chase grinned. "Oh, definitely! Congratulations."

Mark T. kept grinning, but still looked a little confused, as if he'd never, ever thought Chase would admit a noble defeat. There was something smug in that grin, but also something... satisfied. As if proving he was better than Chase was never the goal, but getting Chase to admit he was better at something was actually the goal. And that meant that Chase's opinion actually really mattered to the big ol' bully.

Lucky looked incensed, and Arren took the opportunity to brush him down and give him a big hug. Kassie grabbed his hand in both of hers and shook it fiercely with, "You gave it your best shot!" Then they all cheered his defeat, and promised he'd win next time.

But Chase simply smiled. He felt like he'd won something more important already – Mark T. was finally beginning to make sense to him.

***

It was their weekly meeting with their mother. No one else was around this time. No Costa, no Flannigan. Not even the governor general of Australia. Just their family including

Arren, and their pet which was Random who was, incidentally, practicing being potted flowers the whole time.

"There have been no incidents in the week since the Caretaker left this world, which is either very good news, or very suspicious," Elizabeth informed them.

Arren sighed. "I'm keeping my sensors out, but yeah, all pretty quiet."

"The universe wishes it," Dad informed them with a sage nodding of his head.

"I don't think–" Mum began to disagree, but then there was a knock at the door.

Chase reached out on intuition, always trying to know who was around, but whomever it was at the door was really, really difficult to read. It felt to Chase like they were no threat, but he could tell nothing more at all, which was very unusual.

Simultaneously Chase, Lucky and Arren went to the door and Chase opened it.

Just beyond stood a tall boy. A very, *very* tall boy. He had white hair and wore nothing more than a loincloth. And his very tall skin was very, very blue. It was Moya, whom they'd met on another planet while hiding from a hunting robot, at least until Lucky asked one Moya to lie for him, and they'd all chased them off the planet with torches and pitchforks.

"Oh, hey ya, Moya!" Lucky said with a huge grin. "Won't you come in?"

The boy looked relieved. He was about their age, but so tall he had to duck in to enter the room. He was from a planet with very low gravity. It had been a fun planet, until they had to flee for their lives. And now he was here on planet earth. He looked exhausted, as though he'd been struggling against double gravity for days.

Mum and Dad made room, and Moya struggled to the couch and flumped down, clearly a lot harder than he'd meant too.

"Dude, you look a mess," Lucky said.

"My journey has been most difficult," the blue boy replied.

"How did you get here?" Arren wondered.

"More importantly, what are you doing here?" Mum asked.

The boy smiled, and reached out to hold Lucky's hand. "My friend, you have to come back. Our king is dying..."

About the author

Dr Joe (AKA Dr Joseph Ireland) is a science educational specialist operating out of Brisbane, Australia. He has a wife, three daughters, and a flute. He enjoys playing Dungeons & Dragons with friends and has written award winning fiction for the *Living Greyhawk* series. His true passion is in understanding and promoting scientific ways of thinking in society, having lectured in Science, Technology and Society at Queensland University of Technology.

If you're looking for an exciting science show for your school why not visit www.DrJoe.id.au to find out more!

I LOVE SAMANTHA!

Book 5
Moiya

A desperate plea from another world reaches Lucky and Chase – will they arrive in time to save Rlaeiul's planetary leader from a self-imposed doom? Or will Lucky's love of magic and mischief get them into more trouble than they ever knew was possible. Besides, it's not like the Universal Unity is going to allow them to travel backwards in time to ride dinosaurs... would they...?

Space Chase: Moiya is the 5th book in Dr Joe's "Space Chase" series that explore sound scientific concepts through a fun and engaging narrative. Learn about life on earth, evolution, adaptation, and how to ride a dinosaur as Lucky, Chase, and their alien friend Arren save someone else's world!

Place your mark here each time you read this book!

Feedback and comments are always welcome Arren@drjoe.id.au

www.ingramcontent.com/pod-product-compliance
Lightning Source LLC
Chambersburg PA
CBHW050314010526
44107CB00055B/2235
9780648494164